Creating a
Culture of Learning

Creating a Culture of Learning

Moving Towards Student-Centered Learning

Glenn Meeks

Rowman & Littlefield
Lanham • Boulder • New York • London

Published by Rowman & Littlefield
A wholly owned subsidiary of The Rowman & Littlefield Publishing Group, Inc.
4501 Forbes Boulevard, Suite 200, Lanham, Maryland 20706
www.rowman.com

16 Carlisle Street, London W1D 3BT, United Kingdom

British Library Cataloguing in Publication Information Available

Library of Congress Cataloging-in-Publication Data

Meeks, Glenn.
  Creating a culture of learning : moving towards student-centered learning /
Glenn Meeks.
      pages cm.
  Includes index.
  ISBN 978-1-4758-1277-0 (cloth : alk. paper) — ISBN 978-1-4758-1278-7 (pbk. :
alk. paper) — ISBN 978-1-4758-1279-4 (electronic) 1. Student-centered learning.
2. Effective teaching. I. Title.
  LB1027.23.M44 2014
  371.39'4—dc23   2014021088

Printed in the United States of America.

Contents

Preface

I am quite surprised where I have ended up with this process. Immediately out of college I earned a living as a musician, and then worked as a systems engineer on the contracting side of the construction market for seventeen years. First with small- to medium-sized audio systems progressing to extremely large audio/video/custom control systems (Disney/MGM) and very large integrated access control and video surveillance security systems (Honolulu International Airport).

An educational facility planner convinced me that K–12 school districts could use someone with my skill sets and I have worked on the owners' side of the market as a technology consultant for twenty years. Those projects include: a small, seventy-student K–12 facility for a Native American Inuit tribe on an island in the Bering Sea, located nineteen miles from the Russian border all the way up to a 260,000-student district with a $4.3 billion construction program and everything in between. I have been involved in the implementation of more than $1 billion of technology systems and components.

The foundation of this "Creating a Culture of Learning" process was developed a while back, originally focused more on technology integration. I had developed a Technology Master Plan process modeled after the short timeline and intense, interactive, and collaborative design process used in the architectural world called "design charrettes." I also combined the charrette concept with community consensus strategic-planning strategies. While I had success with a number of those planning processes, the end result was frustrating.

There were a series of large technology-implementation projects where the technology planning and implementation was successful but only a minority of the school district faculty actually integrated the new technology into their instructional process. Why install technology if it is not going to be utilized by the teachers? What a waste of taxpayer funds.

That frustration drove me to ask questions regarding changing how teachers use technology in the instructional environment. What are all of the areas of interest, policies, and processes within a K–12 school district that had impact on learning and teaching? It became apparent that the professional development side of the process was missing, so I created a professional development division within my firm. I hired a former educator with a background associated with integration of technology in the classroom to lead that division. My Technology Master Plan now included aspects of learning and teaching, professional development, and the policies and processes that impact the integration of technology into the instructional environment.

The original concept of multiple silos explained later in this book and facilitating the creation of connections and conduits between those silos was developed at that time. The primary focus of the planning process was the integration of technology into the classroom instructional environment. I had a few successes with the process and a couple of outright failures, which taught me a lot about how to ensure that change actually occurs.

A few years prior to that point, I had started an endeavor to rebuild my company because I found the company interfering with my relationship with my wife. Unfortunately, the rebuilding effort had the unintentional effect of reducing income to a level where I could not sustain development of the planning process. Eventually, I was forced to completely shut that operation down and work as a single-person firm. Most people at that time knew me only as a technology consultant, writing specifications and providing contract administration of technology contractors, so the planning process was shelved.

A few years ago, I had the fortunate opportunity to work with a school district and architectural team to plan and design a Science, Technology, Engineering, and Math (STEM) middle-school project. Every student would have a computing device and teachers would be required to use student-centered learning methodologies. I was challenged to reassess how technology would be used in that instructional environment. Additionally, the school district was so small that they did not have a director of technology and I was challenged to determine how the district would support this new technology environment.

At that point, I delved deeply into public and private cloud computing, high-density/high-speed wireless networks, and various interactive technologies. At the same time, I researched what standardized technical credentials were available and should be required for technology support personnel to ensure they would be capable of maintaining this intensively technological environment. That also made me process and consider: what level of technology literacy would both the teachers and students need to function in that environment? How would they be enabled to obtain that knowledge and those skills?

It became apparent that the key to assisting teachers change how they deliver instruction is not a technology planning process but a planning process focused on learning and teaching.

Shortly after that point in time I was presented with another opportunity with a school district where they would replace 80 percent of their elementary- and middle-school instructional spaces over a three-year span of time. There were multiple architectural firms involved and the district would benefit from a coherent planning process that required each of the architectural/engineering teams to use a common technology standard for their designs.

While the state had a set of school facility design and construction standards, those standards did not address twenty-first-century learning. The facility standards also did not reflect how twenty-first-century learning drives professional development or technology. The state Department of Education did have standards and initiatives regarding twenty-first-century learning but the facility standards did not tie directly to those standards. Therefore, the work of the architectural/engineering teams did not tie back to the Department of Education standards.

I dusted off my Technology Master Plan process and attempted to drive the whole planning process from a student-centered learning viewpoint. The planning process itself worked well. The resulting document reflected the needs of the district using the new instructional spaces as a pivot point to realign their learning environments to a student-centered learning orientation. I also aligned the professional development needs of the district to the new instructional spaces.

While my involvement with that project was winding down, I attended a symposium at a "Net-Zero" facility (a facility that generates more energy than it consumes from the electrical power grid, only if it is not open in the summer and the power generated during the summer is sold back to the power company). The project was designed to also demonstrate a student-centered learning environment. It is a middle-school facility with a principal and faculty specifically selected to demonstrate what student-centered learning should look like. It is a wonderful example of how things should work for students and teachers in today's learning environment.

Even though it was a wonderful demonstration project, I experienced a sense of frustration. This unique project represented one facility out a total of thirty or so in the school district. It struck me that we have a number of demonstration projects around the county where the students are knocking academic achievement out of the park using twenty-first-century methodologies. Yet, those projects typically succeed because of unique leadership at those facilities, not because of changes in the overall learning and teaching culture within a school district. Once that unique leadership leaves the facility, the project will wither on the vine because the district has not changed its policies and processes to support that new environment.

I would express my frustration as follows: We have enough student-centered learning demonstration projects with supporting data to know that the basic concept works well. What we do not have is enough district-wide, all-grade-level, all-content-area demonstrations of student-centered learning. I question the need for more demonstration projects and would suggest that we need demonstration districts. The successful demonstration projects have shown us what can be accomplished; now it is time to execute those concepts on a district-wide basis.

Fortunately, around that same time I was requested by a school district to interface with its cabinet and Board of Education regarding their concern that the district lacked a vision of where technology was heading in the next five years. Given all of the changes in thinking I had experienced over the prior year and a half, I agreed that it was a valid concern but not the real issue. The real issue was that the district lacked a vision of where its learning was headed in the next five years. If it could develop a vision for where its twenty-first-century learning is heading, then the technology should be driven from that vision. It is not about technology, it's about learning and "the student experience." They agreed and engaged me to develop what I called at that time a "Learning and Teaching Road-map" for the district.

One of the more interesting aspects of the project is that the district was at the end of a four-year process where it replaced or remodeled all of their instructional spaces, which included a major technology upgrade. Every instructional station in the district had a teacher laptop, a large-screen projector, interactive whiteboard, infrared microphone systems and speakers, some student response systems, adequate AC power, and upgraded heating ventilation and air-conditioning (HVAC) system. The district also upgraded their data network and added wireless access capability. The five-year roadmap I would generate for the district did not need to address any facility or technology upgrades; it was purely about twenty-first-century learning.

Over the four months it took to execute the project, the superintendent and cabinet observed, made comments, and assisted me as I made a fairly radical transformation in my vernacular. I moved from a technological-based vernacular to a twenty-first-century-learning vernacular in both spoken and written communication. The end result is the purpose of this book, though I will be the first to state that I have much more to learn and understand. Each time I execute this planning process, I gain deeper understanding of how to facilitate the process and aspects of learning and teaching that change various concepts contained within the process.

It was also a journey for the superintendent, cabinet, board members, principals, and teachers who participated in the planning process. It took a while, but the concept "It is not about the technology, it is about learning" finally became the primary focal point. Thinking of technology as today's version of the No. 2 pencil of old, available everywhere and used whenever and however the student needs to use it, represented a major shift in thinking. The most encouraging aspect of the project was that I watched members of a district, from the executive level to the classroom level, change their thought processes and approach for how they plan to educate their students over the next five years. They started the process of changing their learning culture.

Part of the process enables the planning participants to recognize and identify what they perceive to be the hindrances and obstacles to creating a student-centered learning environment/culture within their district. Within sixty days of completion of the project, the district had addressed and successfully resolved three of the four issues the planning participants identified as "high impact" issues. Even though I facilitated the process, the planning participants owned their "Learning and Teaching Roadmap."

As a consultant working to assist K–12 school districts transition to student-centered learning, there is no larger compliment than my clients saying, "Thanks, we will take it from here." They take ownership of the process and substantive changes occur in the district that reflect a transition to a student-centered learning culture without me being the key change agent. Obviously, at best a consultant can be a change catalyst but it requires a core group of people within the district to act as change agents.

As mentioned earlier, I first thought of my process as one where we are creating a "Learning and Teaching Roadmap." As I have executed the process, I realized that the phrase was inadequate. Yes, the process does yield a five-year roadmap of how the district will transition from where it is to a point further down the continuum of twenty-first-century learning. That is what makes the process valuable to the districts that have used it.

However, that is the tactical aspect, the logic and sequence of a number of steps the district needs to execute, not the strategic focus of the process. As I wrote this book and executed the planning process one more time, I realized that I have a major bias that drives all of the concepts herein. The bias is that student-centered learning (with its wide variety of flavors) is much more effective regarding improvement in student academic achievement than teacher-centered learning (didactic—teacher as information gatekeeper). That bias has been created by reading white papers and attending presentations on student-centered instructional delivery methodologies (PBL, IBL, STEM, flipped classrooms, etc.).

The data from student-centered learning studies, when compared to traditional teacher-centered learning, can be startling. The data very heavily favors student-centered learning. Within this preface I have intentionally interchanged the phrases "student-centered learning" and twenty-first-century learning. In my opinion, they are the same.

In reflection of that bias, the primary function of my planning process is to create movement of the district's learning culture from where it exists today to a more student-centered learning culture. My assumption is that the movement will have a positive impact on student academic achievement. The title of this book more accurately reflects what the process accomplishes, *Creating a Culture of Learning*, meaning a student-centered learning culture. I include a very wide range of instructional delivery methodologies as part of that culture.

This is not an academic book utilizing data and analysis to support a specific conclusion. Intentionally, when I express a concept like student-centered learning without citing numerous studies, I am assuming you have also been exposed to the abundant data and there is no need for that argument. To the best of my knowledge, I have only made that type of an assumption related to student-centered learning and Total Quality Management (TQM) and specifically TQM for knowledge-based organizations.

Always keep in mind that I am a systems thinker with an engineer's slant, wanting to understand where the rubber meets the road and real work happens. I am also highly biased toward defining the outcome expected from a process. I then want to define some methodology that measures the outcome to ensure that the process is delivering as expected. I find I am interested in theoretical concepts up to a limited point. If I cannot see a clear path to how the concept affects my clients or how my client can measure the results, the concept has no value to me.

I will also admit that well-constructed vision or mission statements without a set of metrics we can use to measure whether we are adhering to the vision are nice, but of little value to me. I am outcome oriented and hope you will find the process outlined herein valuable to your transition efforts, assisting your district to reach its goals for *Creating a Culture of Learning*.

Introduction

When people ask what it means to *Create a Culture of Learning*, the best definition to date is: it is an internal strategic-planning process facilitating movement toward district-wide student-centered learning. A typical response from participants is that the process is much more comprehensive in scope than they ever imagined. The process touches on issues and makes connections between issues that were not even categories the participants considered important to student-centered learning. The "Best Practice" subjects discussed during the planning process, and covered herein, are specifically selected to focus attention on their district and where on the continuum of the practice does their district currently stand. It then develops goals and strategies designed to "help things go right."

There is another set of concepts underlying the entire planning process. Those concepts can be summed up in three key words: Effective, Efficient, and Sustainable. Specifically applied to public K–12 education, they mean:

Effective—The plan should be effective in increasing student academic and civic achievement. If the plan does not have a positive impact on student achievement, it is a waste of everyone's efforts.

Efficient—The plan should increase teacher efficacy through ensuring teacher "time on task" is focused on student academic and civic achievement. Teachers already have too many seemingly conflicting demands on their time. Can we clarify the expectations placed on teachers, align them with student achievement, and move as many of the activities into automated processes as possible while enabling them to meet state and federal reporting requirements?

Sustainable—The plan needs to address district policies and processes to make the changes driving increases in student achievement and teacher efficacy sustainable. We need to take into account all of the other areas of work within a district and the district policies and processes that impact those two areas. Can we identify hindrances and obstacles and develop strategies for addressing or changing policies and processes, aligning them with the goals of being effective regarding student achievement and teacher efficacy? Long-term, sustainable changes require change in the culture of the district.

As you work through the book, the structure may seem odd in that strategic and tactical aspects of the planning process are contained in one book. It is intentionally designed to meet two specific goals. One, it outlines the core strategic concepts of creating connections between multiple areas of interest within a public education organization. The result is a coherent, comprehensive approach to changing your school district from a teacher-centered to a student-centered culture of learning. Two, it is a tool for use by those public school districts with limited resources to develop their own internal strategic plan. The book is divided into part I, the strategic aspects of the process, and part II, an explanation of the tactical, how do you do it yourself.

The number of small educational organizations with limited resources is much larger than most people realize. Subsequent to a presentation of the strategic concepts of the plan, a school board member was very enthusiastic and inquiring what it would take to facilitate the process in their district. The response caused that person to deflate. They proceeded to explain that they were a school district with only 1,500 students and did not have that level of discretionary resources available in their district. U.S. Department of Education data indicate that there are 13,600 public school districts in the United States (year 2010–2011). Of that total; 6,300 have one thousand or fewer students and another 3,224 serve one thousand to 2,400 students. At least 70 percent of the public school districts in the United States would fall into the organizations with limited resources category. Therein lays the rationale behind mixing strategic and tactical in one book.

Prior to diving into part I, there is a need to assist all readers with the orientation of their thought processes and establish a common language. Chapter 1 suggests primary factors that are driving the first systemic change in public education since the 1890s. That change requires teachers to move from a teacher-centered to a student-centered instructional delivery model. It also provides a cursory summation of research on how people learn and specifically how current students learn. It clarifies the phrase student-centered learning and expands on the concept, inserting "twenty-first century" in the phrase. It provides a definition of what "student-centered twenty-first century" means, suggesting six groups of elements that in combination define the phrase. It concludes with a more detailed delineation of the elements contained within each of those six groups.

Part I starts with chapter 2, providing an overview of the components of the strategic planning concept. It identifies seven areas of interest, or "silos," addressed by the planning process. It also introduces the concept of a coherent approach by aligning the total process to one central silo titled "What/How Students Learn." All aspects of planning for the other six silos should reflect the key concepts of the central silo. Anything that does not advance or build upon the key concepts of the central silo has little value to the overall plan and should be excluded from the plan. Execution of the plan without addressing all of the silos will typically result in the failure of the planning initiative. The chapter also provides an overview of the strategic planning philosophy and definition of the organization members who should be engaged in the planning process.

Chapters 3 through 9 individually work through a set of best practices associated with each of the seven silos. The best practices have been gathered from a number of sources including observed best practices from educational organizations, twenty-first-century business-management concepts, and internationally recognized standards and guidelines. Some are a compilation of all three and others were created in response to specific goals of prior clients.

Within each chapter there are important concepts introduced and explained, and rationales provided for why the concept should be considered important. It is complex, touching many different silos within the organization and requiring the creation of connections between specific silos. Many of those connections are also outlined in their respective chapters. Taken as a whole, these seven chapters provide an extremely comprehensive and coherent overview of what a school district needs to do in order to create a twenty-first-century learning culture for the majority of the students.

Readers will find a small slice of the tactical (how to execute the planning process) at the end of each of those six chapters. There is a list of questions, reflecting the best practices of the chapter, which are suggested for use by the school district that desires to execute the planning process itself. The questions provide a baseline for assessing how far down the road your district has progressed and where the gaps are.

Chapter 10 starts part II of the book, providing a description of how to execute the planning process. There is an overview of the planning process which would be of value to those who want to gain basic knowledge of the planning process but have no interest in the details of how to conduct the process. At that point, feel free to skip the remainder of chapter 10 and all of chapter 11, moving directly to chapter 12, the conclusion.

Those who are interested in executing the process will find chapter 11 to be a detailed description of the planning processes and activities utilized to acquire user input used in generating a planning document. The first section addresses the expertise required by the facilitators and moves on to the data to be gathered prior to the first meetings. It then proceeds with a description of four stages of the planning process: assessment, participant definition of where they want to go, participant development of goals and strategies of how they will get there, and how do the participants define success.

Chapter 11 provides a description of how the participant input is utilized to create a document. It suggests how to use the assessment data and the best practices that seemed to resonate with the participants. It then describes how to assemble the roadmap section, which includes goals and strategies for addressing issues as identified and prioritized by the planning participants. It includes a five-year timeline of activities, along with the operating and capital budget impact of those activities. It finalizes the document construction with reconciliation of revenues and costs and the participants' definition of success. The chapter concludes with the description of a successful document-review process.

The conclusion provides a recap of the salient points of the strategic-planning process and addresses a number of expected responses regarding the concept.

Chapter 1

Establishing Common Language

There are three high-impact drivers of change for the public K–12 instructional environment in the United States and they are part of the federal No Child Left Behind (NCLB) waiver process. The NCLB waiver system was created after it was realized that Phase III targets of the original NCLB, all students at grade level in math and reading by the 2013–2014 school year, were impossible for any school district to reach.

An oversimplified explanation is that to make application for a NCLB waiver there are three primary changes each state Department of Education would need to adopt: a new, more academically rigorous curriculum that also includes the 4Cs (defined later in the chapter); agreement to annual use of online student assessments tied to the new curriculum; and agreement to create new teacher- and principal-evaluation systems.

The states could agree to align their curriculums to the goals of the Common Core Standards, an initiative coming from the National Governors Association and the Council of Chief State School Officers, or create their own. At last count, forty-five states and the District of Columbia have become signatories to the Common Core Standards (CCS—the word "State" is dropped in most references). The states of Alaska, Iowa, Minnesota, Texas, and the Commonwealth of Virginia have created their own standards, similar but different from the CCS. To simplify things, this book uses Common Core Standards (CCS) in reference to the new curriculums, even though each state adoption has variances in how they adopted the CCS or developed their own curriculum.

The new assessments create a number of challenges for school districts. The first is that they must be real-time and online. There will be some wiggle room for the first few years to use paper but that will go away. The other is that the assessments are not simple multiple-choice responses; they are much more aligned with current assessment methodologies.

The new teacher and principal evaluations required regardless of CCS adoption or not are annual evaluations with two primary criteria of equal weight. One-half of the evaluation must be based on student achievement: the test scores of the students taught by that teacher or attending that principal's school. The other half of the evaluation relates to the instructional practices utilized by the teacher in the classroom. Perhaps others will have a different opinion, but the criteria they use for instructional practice evaluation appears to be what I would call student-centered twenty-first-century learning and teaching concepts and processes. Principal evaluations are based on students' academic achievement and how many teachers utilize student-centered twenty-first-century learning and teaching concepts.

The primary point to understand is that for both teachers and principals, an evaluation classifying the individual performance as "Inadequate" three years in a row requires the state Department of Education to place the license of the teacher or principal in jeopardy. Now that we have the primary "drivers" of why change is occurring in educational organizations, we need to discuss some fundamental aspects of our educational environment and a deeper overview of factors driving change.

We cannot discuss instructional processes in the K–12 environment and current knowledge of how people learn without starting with Bloom's Taxonomy from 1956.[1] Specifically, educational organizations have connected with the "cognitive" portion of his map for how people learn. A major concept that readers need to understand is that Bloom outlines a progression for how a learner moves from Lower Order Thinking Skills (LOTS) to Higher Order Thinking Skills (HOTS). A former student of Bloom's, Lorin Anderson, and his associate, David Krathwohl, expanded on and made a few modifications to Bloom's LOTS to HOTS progression.[2]

Essentially, they changed the words Bloom used as the primary indicators of concepts behind cognitive growth from nouns to verbs.

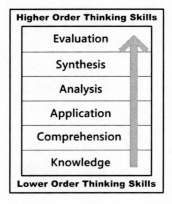
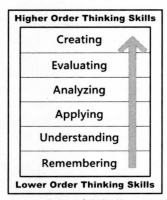

Anderson & Krathwohl

They also flipped the order of the top two concepts. A number of people who understand Bloom's Taxonomy in depth point out that this "Revised Bloom's Taxonomy" from Anderson and Krathwohl is at the center of the new CCS. The diagram provides an overview of the original Bloom concept compared to the Anderson-Krathwohl revision.

Based on a number of comments and articles regarding the Revised Bloom's Taxonomy, an oversimplification of progression would be: You must first *Remember* the facts regarding a concept before you can *Understand* the concept. Then you can determine how to *Apply* the concept and correctly *Analyze* the outcome/results. At that point you *Evaluate* the outcome/results and how they build on what you do and do not know. Only after all of those steps, you are now at the point where you may be capable of *Creating* knowledge.

A simpler, and perhaps easier to remember, description of that progression was developed by Dr. Michelle Selinger and presented by Michael Stevenson from Cisco.[3]

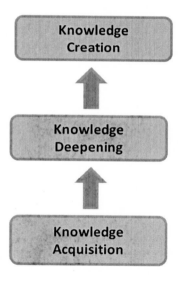

The learner first experiences *Knowledge Acquisition* and then moves to *Knowledge Deepening* and only then can they move to *Knowledge Creation*.

This is a very important aspect of learning and is reflected in the new CCS. The CCS also have a higher level of academic rigor than the curriculums it is replacing. Studies by the state of Ohio's Department of Education suggest that the difference in academic rigor between the old

Ohio standards and the Ohio new learning standards (their adoption of the CCS) is 35 percent. To put it differently, if your third-grader scored a 70 on reading comprehension under the old learning standard, her score would be a 45.5 under the new learning standard. Granted, knowing facts are LOTS but they are the foundation to learning.

The one other aspect of the CCS we need to discuss are the twenty-first-century skills as outlined by The Partnership for 21st Century Skills (P21), www.p21.org. The partnership represents a large and highly diverse collection of people, companies, and organizations who advocate for twenty-first-century readiness for every student. As the United States competes in a global economy that demands innovation, P21 is focused on assisting educational organizations to fuse the skills people need to succeed in that twenty-first-century economy into the instructional process. Development of these twenty-first-century skills is infused throughout the CCS standard for all grade levels and content areas. Most people refer to them as the 4Cs:

- Critical thinking and problem solving
- Communication
- Collaboration
- Creativity and innovation

It may be of value to take a short sidebar to eliminate some potential confusion. The term "4Cs" appears in some of the diagrams and text on the "P21.org" website. Other locations on the same web side only list 3Cs. Sometimes they use communication and collaboration together. Whether you use 4Cs or 3Cs, they are the same thing within the context of this book.

The Revised Bloom's Taxonomy clearly indicates that remembering facts is foundational to the learning process. If the learner cannot remember a concept, he or she cannot progress from LOTS to HOTS.

The new CCS also reflects concepts associated with how students learn in today's digital environment. Marc Prensky has succinctly articulated a generational difference, appropriately called a "big discontinuity," between today's *Digital Natives*—people who cannot remember a time without digital technology—and *Digital Immigrants*—those people who remember a time when there was no digital technology.[4]

Today's students do not match the teacher-centered educational environment based on educational concepts of the 1890s and early 1900s ("The Committee of Ten" from the National Educators Association, Dewey and the Carnegie Foundation as the more recognized contributors). Research indicates that today's students have a preference for a visual-spatial learning mode; learning in more, smaller bits; monitoring several dimensions at once rather than depth with one dimension; need for interactivity and collaboration as meaning-making structure; and different expectations of how they access and interact with each other and information.

The CCS clearly indicates that a "student-centered learning environment," where students hold discussions with each other and the teacher, participate in hands-on projects, and teach their peers is the preferred delivery system for acquiring knowledge versus the twentieth-century "teacher-centered learning environment."

Let's clarify the term "student-centered learning" at this point. There seems to be some confusion regarding the definition of "student-centered learning." Some reference materials describe it as a process where the students determine what they study. Other materials describe it as a highly organized, structured, and directed process, focused on specific content, facilitated by the teacher with learners engaged in a variety of activities. When the phrase "student-centered learning" is used within this book, refer to the latter: an organized, specific-content-focused environment where the teacher is the facilitator of the student experience.

Many educators have pointed out that the CCS reflect that version of student-center learning: expecting learning to occur through organized student experiences rather than teacher activities. Again, the teacher-evaluation systems also seem to hold teachers accountable for using these student-centered-learning instructional delivery methodologies, processes, and concepts.

There are a number of instructional delivery methods that fall in the category of "student-centered learning" environments and all are included without any ranking in efficacy of academic outcomes. This planning process is not a tool for selecting your instructional delivery method. For the purpose of creating a culture of learning, it is more important that the district chooses the delivery method or mix of delivery methods that best fits the district's needs and culture.

Your student-centered learning focus may be project-based learning, interdisciplinary project-based learning, inquiry-based learning, flipped classroom, STEM, STEAM, constructionist, or learning communities to name just a few, or even a mix of all of the methodologies available today. Once you have your management and assessment systems in place (described in subsequent chapters) and have executed the process for a couple of years, your district will have a baseline of academic performance data. At that point you can create pilot projects to assess if one methodology is superior to another for your students.

It is important that we design how we educate today's student based on data, not anecdotal evidence. This would be an excellent place to

provide data coming from all of the Project-Based Learning (PBL) initiatives and private companies delivering PBL services. There is consistent
data that PBL-based student-centered learning for the content area of
mathematics does not provide the 20 to 30 percent gains in student academic performance experienced in all of the other areas of content. Using
project-based, hands-on learning in mathematics simply does not provide
an increase in academic achievement compared to twentieth-century
teaching methods.

It does not mean that other student-centered instructional delivery
methods would not work for learning related to mathematics. It simply
means that we should not assume that the delivery methods that work
in one content area for a specific set of students will automatically work
for all students. We should always be checking to see that what is really
going on matches our goals for student learning.

The CCS clearly expect technology to be an embedded tool used by the
student. Technology for today's students is more like the No. 2 pencil of
old; simply available when and where the student needs it. Technology
is not taught as a specific content subject but rather something embedded in all activities. It is simply a tool. It is also important for readers to
understand that the modern, student-centered environment could not
function without the use of technology by both students and teachers.
This will sound like a music sample repeated again and again, but the
teacher-evaluation systems also hold teachers accountable for embedding
technology in their student experiences.

The phrase "student-centered twenty-first-century learning and teaching" is a nebulous and ill-defined concept for the administrators and
teachers in most school districts. Everyone would use the phrase and talk
about it but no one could really define what it meant. Student-centered
twenty-first-century learning and teaching is a complex concept containing multiple elements. The following is a simplistic overview of what the
phrase means and will need to be updated and revised in the future, but it
represents a reasonable starting point for establishing a common language.

It seems that "student-centered twenty-first-century learning and
teaching" contains at least six groups of elements:

- New Curriculums—The knowledge and skills students are expected
  to know and demonstrate mastery of
- Twenty-First-Century Skill Sets—The twenty-first-century skills students need to compete in a global economy
- Digital Environment—How deep into the digital experience do you
  expect to go?
- Data-Driven Experiences—Knowing what the student does or does
  not know and planning tomorrow's activity based on that data

STUDENT-CENTERED
21st CENTURY LEARNING

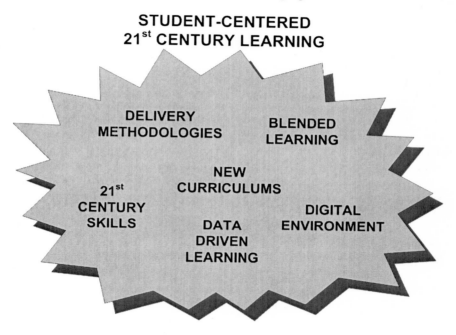

- Delivery Methodologies—How students will gain knowledge or skill sets
- Blended Learning—Where and when will the students gain knowledge or skills?

Everything should focus on the student experience. When talking about the CCS the key focal points are the academic rigor expectations; college- and career-readiness outcomes; student-centered learning activities; and the LOTS to HOTS progression (Knowledge Acquisition ⇨ Knowledge Deepening ⇨ Knowledge Creation).

The twenty-first-century skills are the 4Cs outlined earlier in this chapter. The student experience should enable them to obtain skills related to critical thinking/problem solving; communication; collaboration; and creativity and innovation.

There are three components to your digital environment: digital devices, digital tools, and digital content. How deep into that digital environment do you want to go? Do you wish to create a digital learning environment where students have sufficient access to technology to meet the requirements of their learning experience, including electronic assessments? Or do you want to move to a total digital environment with digital content? Those are two radically different digital environments. Both environments require a complete set of digital tools used by teachers to manage the student-centered learning environment.

The teacher needs to know what his students do and do not know today in order to plan the student experience for tomorrow. Within that data-driven experience environment, the teacher must align the planned student experience to the curriculum; align the experience with student readiness; ensure that the learning experience also contains formative assessment; and use the formative assessment to ascertain if differentiation (intervention/review and advanced activities for gifted and talented) is needed. The formative assessments are also used by data teams and instructional leaders to assess effective and efficient delivery methods and tools making informed decisions based on data.

The delivery method will include student experiences with a mix of discussions, hands-on projects, collaboration projects, virtual field trips, a variety of sources, multimedia projects, students teaching students, individualized learning, connecting to experts and other learners in real time via technology, and one-to-many presentations.

Blended learning means that the student experience should be enabled to occur at a variety of locations on a scheduled or unscheduled basis. Those experiences should be differentiated (students have different primary learning styles); they could be web based; they could occur on campus or off campus; they could be synchronous (occurring with the teacher and other students) or asynchronous (occurring whenever the student needs the knowledge or skill); and technology is used like the No. 2 pencil of old, available when and where students need it.

Creating a twenty-first-century student-centered learning environment for all instructional spaces in an entire district is a very complex process involving many elements. It will be years before twenty-first-century outcomes are the typical experience of every student in the district. This process is designed to enable K–12 educational organizations to start down the path of changing their instructional environment to a student-centered learning orientation.

NOTES

1. B. S. Bloom, *Taxonomy of Educational Objectives, Handbook 1: The Cognitive Domain* (New York: David McKay Co.).

2. L. W. Anderson and D. Krathwohl, eds., *A Taxonomy for Learning, Teaching and Assessing: A Revision of Bloom's Taxonomy of Educational Objectives* (New York: Longman, 2001).

3. M. Stevenson, "Education 3.0 Presentation Notes," Cisco, 2007, http://tools.cisco.com/cmn/jsp/index.jsp?id=73088&redir=YES&userid=(none).

4. M. Prensky, "Digital Natives, Digital Immigrants," *On The Horizon* 9, no. 5 (October 2001) and "Digital Natives, Digital Immigrants, Part II—Do They Really Think Differently?" *On The Horizon* 9, no. 6 (December 2001).

Part I

THE SEVEN SILOS AND THEIR BEST PRACTICES

Chapter 2

Overview of the Process

There are seven silos of interest with multiple issues within each silo that must be considered during the planning process. The term "silo" is a concept developed by business organizational and strategy gurus. It means a department or group of people within an organization that focuses on the needs of their group without consideration or concern about the needs of other groups within the organization. Though it is part of a larger organization, it operates as an independent entity. It would be fair to say that all organizations involving human beings have silos. Some people may call them kingdoms and turfdoms.

Connecting multiple silos within an organization is a complex process. However, if we make a simple and coherent plan from the complex parts, the participants can execute the plan. You make a complex plan simple by defining one overriding concept against which all other issues are measured. Within the creating-a-culture-of-learning planning process the primary concept is:

CURRICULUM/INSTRUCTIONAL
PROGRAM—"WHAT/HOW KIDS LEARN"

Everything about the plan should always focus back to a vision of "What and How Students Learn" within the organization. It is all about the student experience and how learning and teaching affects student academic and civic achievement. The plan should articulate where you want your learning and teaching environment to go and how far down the student-centered learning path the organization wants to progress within the timeline of the plan.

COHERENT PLANNING PROCESS for
STUDENT-CENTERED LEARNING

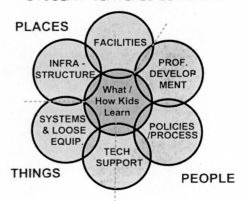

Some questions to be answered are: What student-centered activity/ experience engages the students in effectively gaining core knowledge and twenty-first-century skills? Are they gaining that knowledge and those skills at the appropriate time? What does the instructional structure look like that supports and enables teachers to facilitate those types of activities? Do your students have the academic and technology literacy skill sets that enable them to operate in this environment? If not, how are you going to provide the required remediation?

What resources do your students require based on the instructional activity? Do you have data systems that provide real-time formative assessments which impact teachers' plan for student experiences on a daily basis? Are there friction points in the structure that make it hard to create that student-centered environment? If so, what are your strategies for reducing the friction?

Are these student activities experiences for "Most of the Students, Most of the Time" or "Some of the Students, Some of the Time?" This is the silo that addresses the effective goal of the plan process. The answers to those questions should be the primary reflecting points driving the answers to questions for the other six silos.

PROFESSIONAL DEVELOPMENT

If the students obtain their core knowledge and twenty-first-century skills from learning and teaching practices that actively engage students, what user proficiencies does the faculty member need in order to facilitate those activities? Have we clearly articulated expectations regarding user proficiencies? Does your faculty have competency in twenty-first-century learning methodologies, concepts, and processes?

Does your faculty have the technology literacy skills to facilitate and direct those student activities? Are basic troubleshooting skills for computing devices, network connectivity, and audio-visual (AV) systems included in that technology literacy requirement? How will that faculty member obtain those skill sets and how much will that training cost? What are your expectations of how the teachers manage the student experience process? Has the district converted formative assessments to an electronic format? What tools have you provided to the teachers for managing everything they are expected to do? This is the silo that addresses the efficacy of teachers.

POLICIES AND PROCESSES

This silo represents how you manage people and the systems that are involved in the instructional program. Additionally, this silo and the next four silos address the goal of how we make these changes to a student-centered twenty-first-century learning and teaching environment sustainable.

The issues include: Who is the "keeper" of the formal and informal processes enabling a successful student-centered twenty-first-century learning and teaching program? What "formal communication channels" are in place to ensure policies are followed? How does the local campus staff provide input to the overall learning and teaching functions and decisions? Does your organizational structure reflect today's changes in how teaching, learning, technology components and systems, and technology support are changing within the field of education?

TECHNICAL SUPPORT

How has your vision for effective learning and teaching affected your technical support structure, policies, and initiatives? Does your technical support group respond to district-level instructional requests regarding new technologies with a positive or negative attitude? Are they a hindrance or a barrier regarding your vision for effective learning and teaching?

On the systems side, central to all technical support is the service desk, and the primary question in this regard is do you have an Information Technology Infrastructure Library (ITIL) compatible system? Does your support department practice ITIL-based incident, problem, configuration, change, and continuity management processes? How many technical systems people do you have and what are their specialties? Have they all been trained and hold a minimum ITIL Foundations certification? Do the respective technical job descriptions contain the appropriate Institute of Electrical and Electronics Engineers (IEEE) or Comp/TIA certification requirements?

FACILITIES

While effective and sustainable student-centered twenty-first-century learning and teaching can occur in any existing instructional space, facilities designed specifically for student-centered activities provide a more efficient environment. Are your instructional spaces designed for large-group, small-group, and individual learning-activity flexibility? Does your furniture support a flexible learning space? The traditional tablet armchair does not enable small groups of students to work together.

Are the spaces adjacent to your flexible learning space designed to support student-centered activities? Can the faculty visually monitor those additional support areas? Are the media center and its specialized high-end applications for graphics and audio-video recording and editing extended into those flexible learning areas?

INFRASTRUCTURE

The infrastructure considerations associated with effective student-centered twenty-first-century learning and teaching are primarily focused on the support of the technology used in that environment and specifically related to AC power, cable pathways, and the cooling/heating systems. Are your technology closets zoned so they are cooled separately from their surrounding areas even in winter when the other spaces are being heated? Are those closets designed to the internationally accepted American National Standards Institute/Telecommunications Industry Association/Electronics Industry Association (ANSI/TIA/EIA) standards? Are your primary closets on each campus and your primary district telecommunications rooms prepared and tested for disaster recovery?

Do your technology closets have sufficient AC power for today's remotely powered wireless access points, network cameras, and other devices? How are your closets designed for disaster recovery? Are the cables organized or do they look like a rat's nest? Do all of those cable pathways adhere to the ANSI/TIA/EIA standards? Is there sufficient power in your classrooms to support student devices? Is that power available through USB power hubs for mobile devices?

SYSTEMS AND COMPONENTS

What is the basis for your selection of teacher and student devices? Are they chosen based on your vision for effective, efficient, and sustainable student-centered learning? Are they driven by teacher and student instructional activities and experiences or because they are current and cool technology? Are you using full-blown desktop units for applications that can be run on e-readers or netbooks?

Do you allow your students to Bring Your Own Device (BYOD)? Do you allow the use of cell phones as student response clickers? How do you address the digital divide in your schools between those families with Internet access and computing devices and those without? Are there spaces available before and after school where students can generate their digital homework and where their transportation needs are also met?

Is wireless networking the primary method for connecting all devices to the required resources? Do you have network log-in and authentication as your primary security approach? Does your threat management suite enable BYOD? What other systems are now using the data network as their primary connectivity method? (Voice Over IP phone system, IP video, IP security cameras, etc.) Is your data network capable of supporting this network-centric system approach?

Where are the applications and content used by students stored? Are they on the local device or networked resources? Can students access their storage areas from home? What about teacher storage and backup? If networked, are those servers and applications virtualized? How do teachers connect to their content from outside your network? With the number of student devices increasing in quantity and the potential for digital textbooks on the horizon, what plans do you have for moving to cloud computing?

It is vitally important that all seven silos be considered and integrated into the planning process. A Learning and Teaching Roadmap that leaves one silo out of the discussions and activities will reduce the potential success of the plan by 50 percent. Leaving two of the silos out of the plan virtually assures the plan will never work. It is also vitally important to remember that the answers for all questions associated with the six outer silos should always focus back to and be driven by the answers to the questions surrounding the central silo "What/How Students Learn."

Subsequent chapters will provide more detail to assist readers in understanding the primary concerns for each specific silo.

The actual planning process is fairly straightforward, following a sequence of four questions:

The strategic planning process is not quite so straightforward or simple. Dr. William S. DeJong, an educational facility planner, made the following observation quite a while back.

> There is no reason long-term strategic planning should take a long time to complete. Most strategic plans accurately identify the issues which require resolution at the very beginning stage of the process. Unfortunately, most processes spend ninety percent of their time discussing and debating the ten percent of the issues which cannot be resolved. Therefore, if you can find a way to defuse and set aside the ten percent of the issues which cannot be resolved, you should be able to complete a strategic plan in a very short amount of time.

Completing a Creating a Culture of Learning Plan with Roadmap document should not take more than sixty or ninety days once the process starts. Managing which issues require resolution and those we can defuse and set aside is more about having a clear understanding of the key issues within each silo. There will be politically loaded and unresolved issues from prior events within each district but if they lie outside the boundaries of this roadmap, we can defuse those items by pointing out how they are not within the purview of the planning process.

Dr. DeJong also observed that the types of personnel who should participate in the planning process have changed over the years. In the 1960s, educational organizations were top-down hierarchies, which we all recognize will not work today. You cannot dictate or mandate quality; you can only create an environment where the employees voluntarily participate in the quality-control processes.

In the 1970s, planners moved to "bottom-up" planning processes where the users affected by the changes had a voice in how their business would be changed. That also did not work in educational organizations in that when the governing board or executive cabinet did not agree with the initiatives created by the planning process, they would not fund the initiative, frustrating the users.

He suggested that today's educational organizations need to conduct collaborative planning processes that are horizontal and vertical, including all levels of the organization that have a say in what happens or are affected by what happens. With regard to a Creating a Culture of Learning Plan with Roadmap, the goal is to create an effective, efficient, and sustainable student-centered learning environment for all grade levels in the organization.

That means members of the governing board, executive cabinet, departments, building principals, and teachers should be involved. It should also involve both the brightest, most technologically oriented instructional talent as well as those who approach teaching in the same manner as twenty years ago. If representatives of the policy makers, the management level, and the user level are all together at the same time, no one can say "I did not know/understand." That also starts the process of building a cadre within the district whose members have the same vision for student-centered learning, using the same terms and concepts.

What about the students or parents? Are they not constituents of the district and impacted by this plan? Shouldn't they be involved? The answer is yes, they are impacted by the plan, but no, they should not be involved in the planning process. There are two primary reasons for that statement.

The first is that the roadmap is an internal strategic plan. A truly honest assessment will most likely reveal information that the district does not want the public to know. The planning participants need to understand the assessment and discuss those findings; therefore, the public should not be involved in the planning process. An example: at the end of a major construction project that provided an upgrade of instructional technology in every instructional space, the assessment determined that only 15 to 20 percent of the teachers actually used all of this new technology. After making such a large investment, the last thing the district wanted the tax-paying public to hear is that most of the teachers were not using the new technology installed in their classrooms.

Yet, if the district did not have an honest assessment of where their teachers were at on the student-centered learning continuum, the district would never be able to address the real needs of the teachers. The students would never experience student-centered learning. The district needs the freedom to be honest with itself without worrying about how the assessment data would be perceived by the public.

The second reason is that the roadmap is about the business of the classroom, detailing goals and strategies of how the district will proceed with modifying its business. It is hard enough to facilitate agreement among those people who understand the business. Bringing in people who must be educated about the business and who may have perceptions that do not align with reality creates unnecessary conflict and delay. The public, parents and students, are greatly affected by the outcome of what the district delivers but do not belong in this process.

The following analogy does not work on all levels but it portrays the basic concept. We are greatly impacted by the car product we drive. However, we have no knowledge regarding the business of how that product is manufactured. We are perceptive enough to know if the car performs well or not—handling, acceleration, comfort, quality of the audio system, and so on—but we have no real knowledge as to why it works well.

Parents and students are perceptive enough to know whether students are actively engaged in learning and growing academically but they have no knowledge as to why it is or is not working. We leave the business of making a car to the experts who know the car-manufacturing business. Educational organizations know their business; we will leave the business part of planning for student-centered learning to them.

When you review the Coherent Planning Process diagram with the seven silos, you may have noticed that the seven silos are divided into three broader categories: People, Places, and Things. They represent the three areas of knowledge the facilitator(s) need to have experience in and working knowledge of in order to facilitate the planning process. The rationale for placement of the dividing lines as noted is driven by the belief that one of the ways to divide all people in the world is to have *People* people on one side and *Things* people on the other side of the divide. A *People* person is someone who gains energy by interfacing with other people. A *Things* person finds that other people take energy away, and such a person gains energy by working with things, not people.

It would be unusual to find an individual who has experience in and working knowledge of all three areas *and* has one foot on the *People* side of the divide and the other on the *Things* side of the divide. We have all observed a situation where a person with substantial experience and knowledge in one area attempts to coordinate and direct an initiative that contains operational aspects outside of his personal areas of expertise and experience. The initiative is expected to have a positive impact on other areas but it ends up being much less effective than expected.

If Yogi Berra did not say this, he should have: "They don't know what they don't know." The lack of knowledge and expertise results in gaps in processes and misses critical connections between silos. K–12 school districts around the country are littered with failed or ineffective initiatives. Primarily, they fail because the leader in charge has gaps in knowledge that cause major process inefficiencies or simply render activities ineffective. You must address issues in all seven silos of this coherent planning process.

Chapter 3

What/How Students Learn

You may grow tired of hearing it, but everything about the Creating a Culture of Learning Plan with Roadmap must reflect back to "What/How Students Learn,"the central silo. It aligns all efforts to a singular concept, therefore aligning all efforts with each other. Everything boils down to learning and teaching. The primary focal point of the entire process is the student experience and the outcomes enabled by that experience. As stated in the prior chapter, if we do not provide effective impact on student academic and civic achievement, there is no value in the planning process.

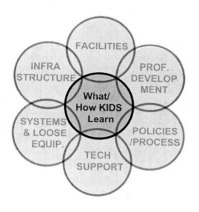

The following are best practices that have successfully resulted in increased student academic and civic achievement. Some are directly derived from observations of successful demonstration projects. Some are from successful district initiatives. Others are a compilation of multiple sources and clarification added from experience. Some reflect overall concepts that have been well documented in other publications and venues.

Mission for Student-Centered Twenty-First-Century Learning and Teaching

In discussions with school district people about a Learning and Teaching Roadmap, the first issue to talk about is the district vision for student-centered twenty-first-century learning and teaching. Does the entire organization—from the executive level, to the departmental level, to the building level, and to the classroom level—talk about student-centered learning in the same way? Does the district have any mechanisms in place that enable the building-level and classroom-level members to monitor how their activities are meeting those expectations? Does the district have mechanisms in place which enable feedback from the practitioners to flow back up to the executive level regarding whether the vision is what happens in the classroom and whether the vision actually works?

It is critical that the executive level has a crystal-clear articulation of expectations regarding student-centered twenty-first-century learning and teaching. One of the cardinal rules of speaking in public is that a concept expressed by the speaker must be crystal clear when expressed from the stage. If there is the slightest amount of fuzziness about the concept expressed by the speaker, the listeners will be in a pea-soup fog. Unfortunately, the typical expression of the district vision for student-centered twenty-first-century learning and teaching is a nebulous, "sort of like," expression. How can classroom practitioners meet expectations regarding their performance when the leaders cannot define those expectations?

A few of the executive-level groups will haul out a well-crafted, district-approved statement that articulates their view of student-centered twenty-first-century learning and teaching, with reams of supporting references. Typically, that document has been authored by the director of curriculum or the curriculum and instruction department. For those readers who fall in this category, there is bad news. Your teachers may have interest in the concepts of the document but they do not use it to govern how they function in their classroom.

The concepts are too large and comprehensive for individuals to hold them in their minds as they function in their classrooms. Brain research clearly indicates that the average person can hold only four or five things in his or her mind at one time. Therefore, the larger and more comprehensive concepts have to be broken down to a few simple but key concepts. Then individual members can be cognizant of those few simple but key concepts as they conduct their business for the district. Does that vision for learning and teaching permeate throughout the entire district?

The concept is not only for the executive level but should also be understood by the members of every department, the building principals and teachers. Do the IT department, instructional technology, facilities, purchasing, finance, and human resources departments pursue their activities with that vision in mind? If so, the entire district is now aligned.

Granted, there are members of the organization whose work the vision will not affect, such as bus drivers, food service workers, and custodians, but the majority of the organization members need to have a clear understanding of the vision. Some readers are raising eyebrows and thinking, "Really?" As we move though the other six silos, the case will be made for why all departments need to understand this vision.

As to the vision itself, the term "vision" for student-centered twenty-first-century learning and teaching is the larger, more complex concept of the cloud with multiple elements as outlined at the end of chapter 1. By definition, a "vision" applies to your view of your organization somewhere in the future.

We need to intentionally change terms. You actually need to create a mission statement for learning and teaching driven by that larger, more complex vision.

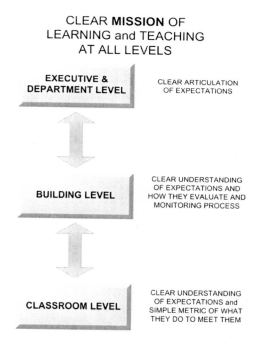

CLEAR **MISSION** OF
LEARNING and TEACHING
AT ALL LEVELS

**EXECUTIVE &
DEPARTMENT LEVEL**

CLEAR ARTICULATION
OF EXPECTATIONS

BUILDING LEVEL

CLEAR UNDERSTANDING
OF EXPECTATIONS AND
HOW THEY EVALUATE AND
MONITORING PROCESS

CLASSROOM LEVEL

CLEAR UNDERSTANDING
OF EXPECTATIONS and
SIMPLE METRIC OF WHAT
THEY DO TO MEET THEM

The mission statement takes the few key and simple concepts and expands them into a set of simple expectations of what makes an appropriate student experience (always focus back to the student experience of learning).

During the first plan facilitated, the facilitator actually generated a mission statement from key concepts the planning participants selected and presented the statement to the planning participants. The statement was simple, straightforward, and easy to remember. Then the language arts people started working on it. The mission statement then became a very nicely crafted expression, but no one could remember the key points of the statement.

If members of the organization cannot remember the key points, they will not be able to use the statement to measure whether classroom activities accomplish the goals outlined by the statement. We do not have anything solid we can measure to provide objective data that the activities match the stated goal. Creating a mission statement is valuable but to accomplish the goal of defining measurable outcomes, the mission statement must be accompanied by a simple rubric. That rubric becomes the definition of the outcomes we use as metrics (measuring points) for the teacher and for quality management by the building principal.

The following is an example of a mission statement and rubric.

> The School District is committed to providing engaging experiences that focus on student-centered twenty-first-century learning and teaching through Critical Thinking / Problem Solving, Communications, Collaboration, and Creativity and Innovation. Staff members have high expectations and create a rigorous academic environment where all students apply grade-level core knowledge and progress to college and career readiness upon graduation.

To make this mission statement a universal concept within the district, the planning participants agreed that every teacher should ask themselves the following simple set of questions regarding every student activity they plan. This rubric should be something all teachers are familiar with and adhere to:

> Is your planned student experience:
> - Engaging?
> - Focusing on twenty-first-century skills?
> - Applying grade-level core knowledge?

Now they have something that can be communicated with every member of the organization and that we can measure. The teacher has a simple, easy-to-remember set of metrics (measuring points) to use every day to determine if the expectations of the organization are being met. Those metrics also enable the building principal to evaluate and monitor whether teachers are conducting themselves as expected by the district, providing quality-control methodologies. Do you see how everything is now focused on the student experience? When the other six silos align their activities to support "student-centered" experiences, we are aligning the entire district to the important issue of "What/How Students Learn."

Equity of Access

You will find that the book presents a thorough argument that a student-centered learning environment requires students to have consistent access to computing devices. If that is so, the question is: what percentage of students has access to a digital environment on a regular basis? Are digital devices, tools, and content available to "most of the students, most of the time?" or "most of the students, some of the time?" or "some of the students, some of the time?" Where on that continuum does your district land?

Are most of your computing devices restricted to computer labs? Or perhaps your district has computer labs with a couple of devices in each elementary- and middle-school classroom. Regarding use of digital devices, that would land you in the middle "most of the students, some of the time." It would also indicate that your district teaches technology as content. That would also suggest your district simply does not have enough student computing devices to use them for instructional enrichment in the instructional space.

If you have reviewed the new curriculums, you have found an expectation that access to technology is embedded in the student experience. Students gain technology literacy simply by using technology embedded as part of the activity that enables them to gain the knowledge or skills they are supposed to master. Technology is not a content area to be covered. Within a student-centered learning environment, access to technology is similar to having access to the No. 2 pencil and paper of old. It is a requirement, not a choice.

To state it in a blunt manner, creating a digital environment requires access to mobile and wireless student computing devices in the classroom. When you start placing more of those types of computing devices in the hands of the students, the student experience changes dramatically. Teachers can no longer stand and deliver; they are forced to engage in a more student-centered learning environment. The rationale behind this statement is located in the digital environment section of this chapter, but it is important to understand that your district does not need to get to a 1:1 ratio of student and student devices to see this effect.

Student experiences delivered through student-centered twenty-first-century learning and teaching methodologies (discussions, projects, etc.) do not require each student to have a computing device 100 percent of the time. Achieving a 1:2.5 device to students ratio will enable a total digital learning environment.

If your teachers are expecting students to accomplish "digital homework" outside of the classroom, how will the district enable that to occur? We all recognize that there is a "digital divide" related to the socioeconomic status of the students' families. Not all students have access to the Internet or computing devices at home. Districts that do not have a large number of student computing devices or mainly desktop, not mobile computing, devices have a harder problem to solve.

If you are one of those districts, do you enable before-school and after-school access to specific areas of the school where the students can work on their digital homework? How does your transportation system enable students to stay late? Do you open your facilities on weekends? Equity of access, including access at home, is a crucial element for student-centered twenty-first-century learning and teaching.

Alignment to Standards

We need to align the student experience to the standards, the standard being the local state adoption of the CCS. For the purpose of discussion, since every state has a different name for their learning standards, and some have developed their own, more academically rigorous curriculums, we will use the term "CCS" as the referral point that actually means your local state adoption of the CCS or new curriculum.

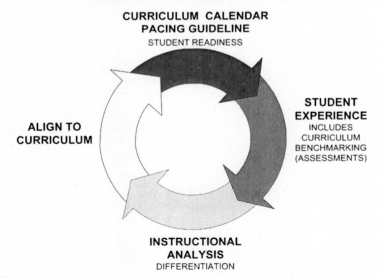

The best practice observed from demonstration schools that have been very successful in gaining high levels of student academic achievement for all students at all grade levels is where they are using *Formative Assessments* to drive tomorrow's instructional experience. You may have heard the process described as "data-driven student learning."

With regard to the student experience, the faculty member runs through this sequence: Does my student activity meet the CCS requirements? Am I on pace to enable my students to learn everything they are supposed to know this year? Are my students ready to learn this material? What student experience am I using to enable the students to learn the knowledge or skills they need? Does that experience have the formative assessments built into the activity? Once my students have completed the activity, do I use those formative assessments so I know which ones can move on and which ones need review? Do I review with the group or only individuals?

This process is a consistent cycle the teacher repeats throughout the school year. If this process is used from the first day students appear at the door of your elementary school, they will meet or exceed academic expectations when they take the state student assessments toward the end of the third grade.

It would be of value to help readers who do not have an educational organization background to understand the difference between the types of assessments performed in educational organizations. The type of assessments as required by the NCLB or state-mandated "End of Grade Tests" are considered *Summative Assessments*. Each is an academic achievement snapshot at a specific point in time where data is used to compare academic results between schools, between school districts, and between states.

As much as this data is used by the politicians and media for comparison purposes, the data has no value for the teacher in the classroom. By the time the summative assessment is made, the academic results being measured may be for student experiences that occurred months or even years earlier. That data is out of sequence in time with regard to providing the teacher with data about what instructional activities the students really need.

Another primary type of assessment used is the *Diagnostic Assessment*, which provides information about a student's prior knowledge and misconceptions before beginning a learning activity. It also applies to a higher-level assessment conducted by a specialist to ascertain individual student strengths, weaknesses, or learning challenges. The information can be useful to a teacher but it does not help to ascertain if today's student experience reached its academic goals.

Formative Assessments take place during a learning activity, in real time, to provide the instructor with information regarding how the learning objectives of a given learning activity are being met. Tomorrow's student activities are based on today's outcomes, ensuring that the majority of the students master the knowledge or skill set of the learning activity before proceeding to the next learning activity. Ongoing formative assessments also provide data for higher-level analysis to ascertain the effectiveness of specific delivery methods.

It is important to recognize that the method for acquiring formative assessments changes based on grade level and content areas. There appear to be two issues. One is related to early-age students where teachers are physically involved in the formative assessments. Reducing the friction involved in accomplishing this task for that age-group of students would greatly increase the efficacy of those teachers. The second is related to the LOTS to HOTS progression. We all recognize that it is much simpler to assess LOTS than HOTS. LOTS are more associated with knowing facts or how to manipulate information to derive a result. We can use multiple-choice questions on a computer and have an algorithm grade a test which measures student knowledge of facts.

However, more advanced content areas require more of a demonstration of HOTS. In addition to assessing the student HOTS capability, how do we assess that the student is gaining the twenty-first-century skill sets embedded in the CCS? Why do you suppose both Scholastic Aptitude Test (SAT) and American College Testing (ACT) have optional essay portions accounting or one-third of the total score? They have developed algorithms that enable software to run an analysis of those essays; the analysis provides a quantitative ranking of the student HOTS.

These discussions are happening among people with much more knowledge regarding the subject matter and understanding of how to measure skills. Both Partnership for Assessment of Readiness for College and Careers (PARCC) and Smarter Balanced Assessment Consortium (SBAC) are working to solve the problem. Even though the College Board (SAT) has solved the machine-scoring problem regarding essays, they do not offer it to the marketplace. Additionally, the industry and users are not far enough down the road to have established indicator standards aligned with LOTS to HOTS or twenty-first-century skills and their machine-scoring applications. Formative assessments of HOTS using machine scoring of student-written documents would be very helpful in today's learning environment. It will be interesting to see where it goes.

However, regardless of how formative assessments are made, it is essential for teachers to know what their students have or have not learned today in order to plan tomorrow's student experience. In today's world, those assessments need to be as electronic as possible.

Learner Profiles

Teachers have known intuitively for decades and now data clearly indicates that different students learn in different ways and at a different pace. No one learns in the lock-step concept of the Industrial School model. Without a doubt, educators would define an effective teacher (one who impacts the academic achievement of students) as someone who knows her students. Unfortunately, each teacher has to restart learning about his students at the beginning of each academic year (primary and middle-school grades) and perhaps semester (high school using block scheduling). We would have a tremendous impact on teacher efficacy if a learner profile were part of each student's Student Information System (SIS) profile.

In the digital environment there are robust learner-profile assessment applications available, and school districts should start student assessments as early as possible and update them on a regular basis. The application should be capable of assessing the individual student learning preferences and styles; the student's types of intelligence; influences based on gender, culture, and personality; and individual student interests. A major friction point in using learner profiles is that none of the learner profile applications talk to the SISes out there at the current time, forcing the teacher to use multiple digital resources to gain a picture of the individual student. However, integration between applications in the near future would be immensely powerful.

Let's take time to explore how learner profiles will assist the typical teacher in the near future. You are aligning with the curriculum and there is specific content or skills your students are supposed to obtain. As the teacher, you group your students by learning profile and plan a variety of student experiences, each delivering an instructional experience specifically aligned to the learning preferences, styles, and so on of each group of students. In your classroom there are now four or five distinctly different student experiences (instructional activities) occurring that have been designed to match the learner profiles of your students. Now we are being effective and efficient.

Unfortunately, there are quite a few obstacles. The lack of connectivity between the learner profile and SIS applications was mentioned in a prior paragraph. The Learning Management Systems (LMS) do not enable classification of the learning activity based on the learning modes, intelligences, styles, and so on that the activity is designed and tested to reach. Sure, they are all "project-based learning" activities, but is one more visual-learning oriented, auditory-learning oriented, or kinesthetic? Is the activity aligned to a specific thinking style? Once we do have that detailed level of data along with connectivity, it opens up a whole other world of learning.

Your district has been using data-driven student learning, learner profiles, and instructional activity classification for three years. You have a student who has "hit the wall" in a specific subject area (it happens to everyone at some point). As the teacher, you run a search for a prior student with a similar learning profile from the same grade level and in the same subject area who hit a similar wall. The search reveals data regarding the instructional activities the prior student's teacher used to assist the student to overcome the learning blockage point. We are now connecting to effective and efficient learning at an extremely deep level. The corporate world would call that type of activity "data analytics."

Digital Learning

There is a major concept we need to explore regarding quantity of student computing devices that has a huge impact on your digital environment. You most likely assume you must move to a 1:1 student to computing device ratio to create a "digital learning" environment, but that is not necessarily true. There is a major difference between creating a "digital learning" environment versus creating a "digital content" environment: eliminating textbooks.

You can create a very productive and engaging "digital learning" environment where all students have access to technology when and where they need it to accomplish specific instructional activities and electronic formative assessments without moving to a 1:1 device-to-student ratio. During planning for a project it became apparent that once you reach a 1:2.5 ratio (one computing device for every two and a half students), in your classrooms, you should have a sufficient number of student computing devices to meet all of your digital learning activities.

Providing that number of devices will also force a major change in how teachers manage their classrooms. The reality is that unless you are eliminating textbooks, you do not need a 1:1 ratio. Perhaps for your district, this is a simpler first step toward student-centered twenty-first-century learning and teaching.

Painting a scenario for you should be helpful. Let's say you have four elementary classrooms with twenty students in each classroom. You provide five student devices in each classroom, enabling small-group collaborative activities or five students to work individually with digital content. There are another fifteen devices on a small cart shared among those four teachers. When the teachers coordinate the cart schedule and a teacher pulls the cart into his or her classroom, every student in that classroom would have a device.

The teachers coordinate between themselves as to who has the cart based on the planned student experience which requires each student to have one. That is a 2.5:1 ratio when you work out the numbers. This concept of a 2.5:1 ratio being adequate will work for any grade level as long as the teachers use a project-based, interdisciplinary instructional delivery program.

Let's expand that concept a little further and see what that means to a district. Let's say that your district has a 5:1 student-to-computing device ratio (six hundred student desktop computers or laptops for three thousand students—not counting teacher, administration, and staff computing devices). You want to move to a digital learning environment. We need to increase the number of devices to 1,200 student computing devices.

The interesting point is that if you are currently at a 1:5 desktop computer-to-student ratio and allocating annual refresh funds to replace old devices, you can get to the 1:2.5 ratio without allocating additional dollars to your computing-device-refresh funds. Instead of purchasing desktop or laptop computers, you use the same dollars and purchase as many netbooks/Chromebooks or inexpensive tablets as you can. Your desktop replacement to Chromebook/netbook ratio will be better than two for one and over your five-year cycle, you will reach the 1:2.5 ratio in five years.

There are a few specific points of how the 1:2.5 ratio actually works. First, there may be a difference regarding how you distribute the devices based on grade levels. The issue is whether you are driving changes in your middle schools and high schools requiring your teachers to move away from a departmental organization structure. Second, you need to eliminate all computer labs that are not serving a specific content area (high school). Stop moving students to a special location and put the technology where the students are.

The primary grade levels typically have students working through all content areas of the curriculum in one room. In that situation, the scenario outlined works quite well. School districts located in parts of the country where campuses are comprised of clusters of classrooms connected by covered walkways will have a harder problem ensuring the shared cart is moved from one classroom to another in a safe manner.

If your middle-school and high-school facilities are departmental, the distribution system described above will not work. If I am an English teacher, either all of my students need a device for today's activities or none of them need a device. At that point, you would need to distribute five carts with twelve devices for every six teachers and the teachers coordinate schedules to ensure they have sufficient computing devices for their scheduled student experience. But again, you can get there in five years using your annual refresh funds.

Creating a digital learning environment is your first step, and there is a phased concept toward 1:1 ratios which may work for your school district and your financial parameters. Your first step, creating a digital

learning environment, establishes the digital tools and information technology (IT) management systems along with the first grouping of digital
devices. Your second step would be to "Go Digital" at your high schools,
providing devices for every student at those facilities and adopting digital
content for those grade levels. Then you do the same thing at your middle
schools, and finally push it down to your elementary schools. That way,
you are not adopting digital content across all grade levels at the same
time, a more onerous task. You are still faced with the task of resolving
how you will address your high-school students who are reading substantially below their expected literacy level.

There is no reason why most K–12 organizations could not accomplish
this task. Once a school district allows BYOD, the students with personal
devices make it an even easier goal to reach. Any organization looking
to move in this direction should create a reasonably sized pilot project
enabling teachers, principals, and IT staff to understand how to use and
manage this new environment.

It is very important to note that simply purchasing the more productive
and less expensive student computing device does not complete the picture. You will need to find funds for implementing a high-density wireless network; see the section on wireless networks in chapter 9. If you are
one of those districts that have cut your refresh funds in order to balance
the budget, funding issues will be the first obstacle you must overcome.

Digital Content

The mission statement with its simple rubric, the data-driven student
learning concept, and the new curriculum with twenty-first-century skills
provide a detailed set of expectations and structure of what students are
expected to learn. What will teachers use as content to meet those expectations? In today's public-school instructional environment, teachers use a
mix of traditional proprietary printed resources (textbooks), proprietary
digital resources (applications), open source resources, and teacher collec-
tions of information both printed and digital.

The majority of teachers organize their instructional activities around
the traditional textbook, using the other resources as supplemental content. The majority of K–12 practitioners acknowledge that those traditional textbook resources have questionable value in meeting the needs
of a student-centered learning environment. As instructional processes
move more toward student-centered learning using discussions, hands-
on projects, and student as teacher, where does a textbook fit into those
processes?

Here is a bias you need to recognize: the textbook industry has not
been astute in how they have addressed a changing market. The textbook

publishers are trying to build protection around their business practices similar to what the recording industry tried to do in the late 1990s. Even today, for many textbooks, you cannot obtain an electronic version of the textbook until you own the physical textbook. Really? How has that worked for the recording industry?

Technology has proven to be a major disruptive force in many industries and it is just starting to really arrive in the textbook publishing market. The textbook publishing industry is in the middle of a major upheaval, especially in the higher-education market. Similar issues will crop up in the K–12 market. It will be interesting to see where everything lands.

Why do the majority of teachers organize their instructional experience around textbooks? There appear to be three primary factors. One is simply inertia. Textbooks have been the primary source of content for decades and the textbook publishing industry is huge. Textbooks are used simply because they are what we have used in the past. A big part of that inertia is also your state department of education and their "textbook adoption" approval process.

The second factor is that teachers have no alternatives. The majority of teachers do not have the time to search for content on their own and then align it to the curriculum. The third issue is an inadequate quantity of student devices available for use as digital textbooks in the classroom and to send home for students. Digital content requires a 1:1 student-computing-device-to-student ratio.

If you are intending to move to a 1:1 computing-device-to-student ratio, we need to talk about the concept of "Going Digital." The concept of Going Digital is from Dr. John R. Kellogg, superintendent, Westerville City School District, Westerville, Ohio. While working as the assistant superintendent of curriculum at another local school district where a Creating a Culture of Learning Plan with Roadmap was facilitated, he developed the concept. It came out of discussions of best practice for a school district moving to a digital environment.

His observation is that the specific concept of Going Digital has three primary components: digital devices, digital tools, and digital content. This is a crucial concept to understand before pushing to a 1:1 ratio. As a side note, the concept of "digital learning" outlined in the prior section does require implementing the first two components, digital devices and digital tools, but retaining the traditional textbook and teacher supplemental information as content. The process of Going Digital, in contrast, eliminates printed content.

Digital devices are those computing devices used by students and teachers. Achieving a 1:1 ratio is very much within the reach of virtually all school districts in the country, once you move to web-browser-type devices and dump textbooks. A definition of "student computing device" occurs in chapter 9 and yes, it will be some type of netbook or tablet. But it cannot cost more than three hundred dollars or so.

In 1998, the Texas Education Agency, which was spending in excess of $1 billion per year in textbooks, commissioned a study on what it would take to replace textbooks with an electronic device for all students in Texas. The conclusion was that devices costing around three hundred dollars per student would enable school districts to use textbook funds to purchase those units without increasing spending. It is interesting that the subject of digital curriculum and moving away from textbooks comes up as a discussion point during the process of facilitating Creating a Culture of Learning Plan with Roadmap.

After working through the issue with a number of districts, it appears that the Texas Education Agency was basically spot-on with their conclusion. Once a district overcomes the initial cost of providing a device to every student, refresh cost for those devices is close to the annual expenditures for textbooks and desktop computer refresh.

Digital tools pertain primarily to those tools used by teachers to create and facilitate the student-centered environment. A more detailed overview of those digital tools is provided in the next chapter, chapter 4. They enable the level of efficiency required to match up to an environment where the academic achievement for every student is tracked on a daily basis. Without these tools, teachers would not be able to manage the student-centered learning environment. A simple list would contain:

- Student Information System (SIS)
- Gradebook (if not part of the SIS)
- Learning Management System (LMS)
- eAssessment System (if not built into LMS)
- Learner Profiling System
- Social Media with Interface to LMS (if not built into LMS)
- Student Data Dashboard

Digital content, the last component of Going Digital, represents the resources used in the student-centered environment that enable the student to gain knowledge or skill sets aligned with the new CCS. This is the one area representing the biggest hurdle for any school district to overcome with regard to moving away from textbooks. In chapter 5 under the funding subsection, a process is outlined where you will have to use the annual funds traditionally set aside for textbooks to purchase a digital device for every student. This is also a source of a bias against what textbook publishers are doing today regarding digital content. If the district has to pay a publisher the same amount of annual funds to obtain digital content as they spent for textbooks, what revenue source do they use for the student devices?

That means you must find digital content that has no or very little cost attached to it. The task of reviewing all grade levels and content areas of your state's adoption of the CCS and finding free content matching the knowledge or skills your students are supposed to obtain is massive.

One school district that went "All Digital" in 2008 was asked how they found the free digital content. The response was: "Brew a bunch of pots of coffee and simply start browsing the free content websites." The question then becomes, who will spend that large amount of time to create the collection, and who will verify that the resource found matches and align to the curriculum requirements? They also cautioned that most of the free content may not be at a quality level acceptable to your district.

We are all aware of the task represented in adoption of new textbooks. The process of adopting digital content is larger. However, everyone will be going through a process of adoption of new resources with the new CCS being implemented in the fall of 2014. Since you already have to make a major effort to change what you already have, replacing your old textbooks, how much larger of a step is it to completely change and move to a total digital content environment?

There are quite a few nonprofit sources working on the digital content problem along with open source sites. There are a small number of school districts across the United States that made a transition to a complete digital curriculum (with the digital content) quite a number of years ago. Many of those school districts are located in states that are signatories to the CCS. Some of them are willing to share their tools for aligning digital content with other school districts at a fraction of the cost for purchasing textbooks.

We are at the very beginning point of schools attempting to move to an all-digital learning and content environment. Once there are more schools moving in that direction, we will have more best practices for digital content to observe and copy. It would be reasonable to expect that digital content in support of the new curriculums will become a major force in the near future.

There is one solution to this problem that we should not ignore. There are a number of companies who are contracting with computing-device manufacturers to build student devices to their specifications. They lock down the operation of the device; it can only perform the activities the company deems appropriate for students. They also extend aspects of the control functions to the teacher device. Simply stated, from a hardware control issue, this eliminates any questions of whether your IT department has the knowledge and skill sets to manage this radically different digital environment with digital content.

The big issue is that the companies are bundling digital content with the devices. They will also allow teachers to add content to their base package. There are a number of early adopters and districts with more flexible funding capacity who are trying out one of these packages as a great tool to jump-start their district toward Going Digital. It enables the district to bypass a large number of issues that must be addressed if they developed everything on their own, and it delivers a student-centered learning environment. A few of these companies will allow you to sub-scribe to their digital content without purchasing their device, another alternative.

It is a very creative solution to a very complex problem but it still comes down to the financial model. The devices fall into the required price range of around three hundred dollars. However, the companies will charge an additional fee for a subscription to the digital content. They make their money from the long-term subscription payment. The combination cost of device and subscriptions will exceed the financial resources available to a majority of the school districts.

Before we leave the concept of digital content we should acknowledge that there are very few school districts that have tackled adoption of digital content for all grade levels and content areas. From the viewpoint of sharing best practices regarding adoption of digital content there is a major gap in how school districts will proceed. There are insufficient numbers of school districts who have successfully implemented digital-content-adoption processes to suggest a specific process as a best practice. It is reasonable to expect that will change over the next few years and per-haps a future update of this book will pull a representative best practice for adoption of digital content into the fold.

Digital Copyrights

Before we leave the subject matter of content, we need to discuss copy-right issues related to education. First, the typical disclaimer: the author is not licensed to practice law and anything stated herein is simply his viewpoint, and readers should seek an opinion from their legal counsel regarding the issues outlined herein.

Copyright law in the United States is a series of legislative acts where each act builds on prior legislation passed by Congress, and interpreta-tions of that legislation are handed down by U.S. federal courts, includ-ing the Supreme Court. Things became much more complicated with the invention of the video cassette recorder (VCR), resulting in a series of lawsuits regarding their use, that were resolved in the Supreme Court in 1984. One of the results of the case was the creation of what is called "Fair Use" practices for copying video content. Things became much more complicated with the technological advance to digital audio and digital video content. In response, Congress passed the Digital Millennium Copyright Act in 1998, which virtually locked down all digital content, eliminating the analog "Fair Use" concepts that had been in use for fifteen years.

In response to the removal of "Fair Use" of digital content, Congress passed the "Technology, Education and Copyright Harmonization" (TEACH) Act in 2002, which addressed digital content copyright with regard to use by nonprofit educational entities and governmental agencies (federal, state, and local). The act also required the Copyright Office of the United States Patent and Trademark Office (USPTO) to hold a conference and generate a report that outlines criteria for how the act is applied and technological solutions for users to meet the conditions of the act.

First, readers need to understand that the TEACH Act does not apply to content generated, licensed, and sold specifically for educational purposes. If your district has subscribed to or purchased digital educational content from a textbook publisher or supplemental content providers like Discovery Education or Schlessinger Media, you must follow the license agreement included with that subscription or purchase. The TEACH Act does not apply to the content of any digital software packages you have purchased.

Outside of content generated by a private firm for educational purposes, all other works are subject to the TEACH Act. The TEACH Act brings a large collection of digital content into the realm of supplemental material a teacher can make available to their students. An example is use of the section from the film *ET* where ET levitates a selection of colored balls of different sizes from a book illustration of the solar system. ET also places them in orbit at the distance and speed associated with how our solar system is aligned. It would be a great way to introduce the concept of the solar system to early learners.

According to the report from the USTPO back to Congress, a nonprofit educational entity or governmental agency can copy, store, and distribute digital content under the following conditions (paraphrased):

- Content is being used as part of a "mediated instructional activity," which means activities directed by an instructor.
- All members of the organization have been educated regarding current copyright parameters.
- Only members of the organization (teachers and students) can access the material. Essentially, it is on your network, behind your public/ private firewall.
- The organization must take technological measures to restrict the users from accessing the information for periods of time longer than the class sessions. As students move up in grade level or to different

classes, their access rights to the material are removed. Your LMS should have that feature.

- The organization must take technological measures to prevent the dissemination of the works by its users to others outside the organization. This is quite simple when using web-browser-based computing devices; there is no storage so the user cannot copy and redistribute the content. When students access the content from outside the district through your access portal, copying of the content is denied by your system.

It is appropriate to point out how the TEACH Act is interpreted is subject to a wide range of legal opinions. Do not take your legal counsel's opinion for granted. You can find legal opinions agreeing with the more liberal application of the TEACH Act as noted above and those that are more restrictive. Part of that depends on who the legal counsel is representing. There are organizations that land on either side, liberal or restrictive interpretations. The most important issue to remember is that there have been no federal court cases regarding interpretation of the TEACH Act and its application in K–12 organizations. There are some cases currently working through the courts regarding universities and Massive Online Open Classes (MOOCs).

However, those are not the application of the TEACH Act as noted herein for K–12. It is of major interest that the Disney Company, the most aggressive of all companies in protecting their intellectual property, dropped all copyright cases against educational organizations after passage of the TEACH Act.

The more restrictive interpretation of the TEACH Act is that it only applies to distance education classes and normal classroom activities are not eligible. However, the Copyright Office of the USPTO makes a very clear point in their report to Congress that the concept of distance learning in a digital environment is different than a physical environment. They clearly articulate that the transmission of data from one classroom to another classroom in the same building is essentially no different than the transmission of data from one campus to another campus. Therefore, they include all classroom activities that are mediated by a teacher as eligible for application under the TEACH Act.

Student Technology Literacy and Fluency

The response encountered when discussing student technology literacy and fluency is "What do you mean, student technology literacy? They know how to manipulate technology better than I do." Valid statement, but it misses the mark. Student technology literacy should mean that students know, appropriate for their grade level, how to use technology in support of a specific student experience. Typically, that would relate to search skills and personal productivity applications (word processing, spreadsheet, graphics/drawing, and presentation). As an example: At what grade level should a student know how to enter data into a spreadsheet? At what grade level should a student know how to create a spreadsheet where others can enter data? At what grade level should a student know how to create an array for analyzing the data in the spreadsheet?

When we take a look at the CCS, student experiences are expected to have technology embedded within the experience throughout the CCS. Unfortunately, this is a radical departure from how most school districts teach technology. Even in the few states that have an actual K–12 technology curriculum defined, technology is taught as a content area. Only one state actively attempts to get their school districts to embed technology literacy development into student projects tied to other content areas.

That is not to say that states and districts are not trying to enable student technology literacy; we are saying that the way most are approaching the issue is not embedded into instruction. It is an instructional goal, which means it is being taught as a content area. How do we know? The answer to a simple observation will inform readers which category their district falls into.

Do your students gain the technology skills they need through spending a specific amount of time in a computer lab working on technology skill activities, or do they obtain their technology skills through activities related to instruction in other content areas? The latter is what the CCS is looking for. To reiterate a concept, today's technology is the No. 2 pencil of old, a tool used during the learning process when and where it needs to be used, not to be taught as a subject.

Granted, like any other area of learning, technology literacy is a building block where we build on prior knowledge and skill. So when do we start embedding technology into the curriculum? We need to take a look at the CCS and the two associated assessment consortiums, PARCC and SBAC. Both consortiums will require online testing, and a few people are starting to catch on that by the end of the fifth grade, students are expected to write a short essay as part of their annual assessment answers.

So if fifth-graders will need to type a few paragraphs as an essay, when should we start teaching them keyboarding? Keyboarding? Yes, there are other ways to input information; we can use a voice recognition system both on computers and smartphones. However, those systems have major issues with noisy environments. Can you imagine what it would sound like to have twenty-five fifth-graders all talking at one time to their computing devices? There are methods for subvocalization, but we cannot reasonably venture a guess as to how long it will be before we have embedded sensors and we can subvocalize and the computing device will understand us.

It would appear that keyboarding will be the default input method for school computing devices for a while. To come back to the original question; what grade level should students start learning keyboarding? The answer is third grade, and you should use one of the "gaming" solutions that teach keyboarding skills. A quick side note: this is a major driver of student computing devices. If we need third-graders to start learning keyboarding as part of instructional activities, this means the student computing device starting in third grade needs to have a keyboard.

There is another factor that has caused school districts to approach teaching technology as a content area. No school district in the United States is held accountable to ensure that students have actually acquired the technology literacy they need to compete in a global economy. Obviously, if a state does not have a K–12 technology curriculum, why would school districts in that state be concerned about a goal no one will hold them accountable for achieving? We are not saying districts have failed in addressing the issue, it is simply that the attempts are disorganized and do not include feedback mechanisms assessing whether the goal is being reached or not.

Even the states with a defined technology literacy curriculum do not measure and publish information regarding how many of a school district's students have or have not met the technology literacy standards appropriate for their grade level. There are no penalties or inadequate performance labels associated with how well the district has achieved the goal of student technology literacy. In the cacophony of things schools are held accountable for, anything without a penalty or label a school district wants to avoid will not be prioritized as a goal to accomplish. Student technology literacy is simply not a prioritized goal.

We need to explore a disturbing reality that adds substantial complexity to the concept of creating student-centered learning environments. We can create the greatest student-centered twenty-first-century learning and teaching classroom you have ever seen, but if the students do not have even basic literacy, they cannot function in that environment. This issue was brought to light through a conversation with a principal of a large high school in a medium-size metropolitan area.

During the discussion about the elements of student-centered twenty-first-century learning and teaching, the principal said, "One-third of my incoming freshmen read at the third-grade level. They would not know how to function in student-centered twenty-first-century classrooms if I had them." The complexity is that your student-centered twenty-first-century learning and teaching process must accommodate those students who are not performing at the academic level of their peers. How do we do that and how do we help them catch up?

If you are successful in creating a student-centered twenty-first-century learning and teaching environment in your school district, you will have a problem similar to but different from the nonliterate students. Not every school district will be successful to the same level of twenty-first-century academic achievement at the same time. You will have students transferring into your school district from other districts who have been less successful. How will you assess where those students are in their twenty-first-century academic progress and technology literacy? How will you enable those students to catch up to their peers in your classrooms?

The section started off with the title of student technology literacy and fluency. What do we mean by student technology fluency? It's similar to the difference between being literate in a foreign language versus fluent. Being fluent means you have higher-order skill sets in the language. In a similar manner, we should define student technology fluency as something of a higher order, where the student exhibits sufficient knowledge and skills enabling self-directed use of technology in support of mid-order to high-order thinking skills.

Before we leave this section on literacy, we need to refer to one other group of people with substantial expertise in this issue. The International Society for Technology in Education (ISTE) and their National Educational Technology Standards for Students (NETS-S), Teachers (NETS-T), and Administrators (NETS-A) have been the standard most states have used as the basis for their K–12 technology curriculum. When you look at the current ISTE NETS-S, published in 2007, you will find that the first four of six areas relate directly to the P21 twenty-first-century skills that are embedded into the CCS.

The fifth area is digital citizenship and the sixth is technology operations and concepts. These are some very high-level descriptions of what students should be capable of with regard to technology. The ISTE also produced "Profiles for Technology (ICT) Literate Students," which provide a bit more illumination of what the NETS-S should look like. However, even within the document, ISTE acknowledges that the profiles should not be considered a comprehensive curriculum.

It will be helpful when a few districts have developed a definition of student technology literacy based on the activities expected from the new curriculum. What explicit technology skills does a student need to execute the student experience suggested by the new curriculum? Once that definition is made, it will enable a district to measure whether their students have the embedded skills meeting the expectations of the curriculum.

As noted in chapter 2, the following set of questions is designed to assist a school district to conduct this planning process and perform a self-assessment. A different set of questions will be posted to the end of each chapter through chapter 9.

Assessment Questions associated with the "What/How Students Learn" Silo

Readers need to first understand the best practices used for each silo before they would understand a series of simple questions to be asked that enables assessment of the district with regard to a specific silo. Readers should also note that to obtain a true picture of a district, the same questions should be asked of members at the executive, departmental, building, and classroom levels.

- Does the district have a vision for learning and teaching?
- If so, can anyone articulate that vision without referring to the document?
- Whose vision is it (where was it authored)?
- Does that vision permeate the organization from executive level down to the classroom?
- Where are most student computing devices located? Labs or typical classroom?
- When excluding teacher, administrator, and high-school content-specific computer labs, what is the computing device to student ratio?
- How does the district enable digital homework for those students without internet access or a computing device at home?
- Do the teachers implement student-centered learning methodologies? What percentage?
- Do the teachers align their student experiences to the curriculum standards? What percentage?
- If so, how is that process managed by the teacher?
- How do teachers assess student readiness?
- Do the student experiences contain formative assessments? What percentage?
- Do teachers use those assessments to plan next-step student experiences?
- Do teachers actively provide differentiation in their classrooms? What percentage?
- Does the district develop a "learner profile" for every student?
- Where does the learner profile data reside?
- Does the learner profile data connect to the SIS?
- Does the district LMS enable classification of student experiences?
- If so, are teachers held accountable to align the student experience with their learners?

- Where along the continuum is the district with regard to developing a digital learning environment?
- What percentage of content resources are digital?
- Do teachers use digital content as part of their student experience? What percentage?
- Does the district have plans to move to digital content and 1:1 device/student ratio? If so, what is the expected timeline?
- Does the district have a definition of student technology literacy?
- How does the district enable students to gain technology literacy?
- How does the district assess that the students have mastered technology literacy?

Chapter 4

Professional Development

When we stop to think about it, the majority of your teachers are digital immigrants. That implies that student-centered twenty-first-century learning and teaching concepts, processes, and technology literacy were not issues when they obtained their professional degree and certification. To help readers understand the size and scope of this disconnect, answer the following question. How many years will it be until we have a digital native (someone born after 1985–1990) as the dean of the college of education at your local university?

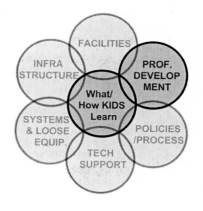

We are not implying that colleges of education are not trying to change and adapt to the new requirements placed on teachers. We are simply stating that the educational training received by the majority of your teachers does not match the new expectations outlined in the CCS. Therefore, school districts now have a task similar to what corporate America has been going through for the last two or three decades; school districts have to retrain their employees.

Additionally, typical of any human organization, there is a wide range of willingness to accept change among the members of the organization. Fortunately, corporate America has developed expertise and processes enabling organizations to change and we can learn from their work. Their research suggests that if you can convince 30 percent or more of the members of an organization to adopt the desired change, the whole organization will change. The goal of a Creating a Culture of Learning Plan with Roadmap is to create a culture and environment that enables 30 percent or more of your teachers to adopt student-centered twenty-first-century learning and teaching concepts and processes in their classroom.

The following are best practices observed that impact the efficacy of teachers. As noted in the prior chapter, these are a combination of direct observations and compilation of concepts from multiple sources including the author.

MULTISTRAND PROFESSIONAL DEVELOPMENT

Most professional-development programs do not recognize the variation of user acceptance to change. Most are fairly monolithic in their approach delivering the same opportunities to all users.

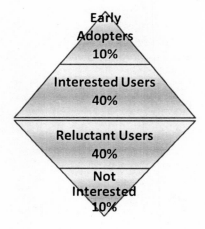

The diagram provides an overview of the typical makeup of any human organization and the division of member attitudes toward change. It is aligned to an educational organization.

Approximately 10 percent of your teachers are Early Adopters. As soon as they see a new thing that they believe will help their students, they completely change their lesson plan and instructional process. Some people affectionally call them crazy because most of their peers think they are crazy for creating that much work for themselves. A caution for readers:

these Early Adopters are typically not the teachers who influence your staff. They are the experimenters who cannot understand why everyone else is not changing along with them.

Members of the next group, the Interested Users, represent approximately 40 percent of your teachers. If you can demonstrate that a specific thing will help their students, they will adopt change but it needs to be demonstrated and structured. These are the teachers who have real influence with the remainder of the instruction staff.

The third group represents another 40 percent of the teachers and they are not really interested in change. However, if the majority of the Early Adopters and Interested Users adopt change and they see that the changes are working, they will adopt change.

The last group, representing approximately 10 percent of your teachers, has no interest in change at all. The teachers in this group may be planing to retire within the next five years or they are simply burned out. You can easily find the 30 percent of total organizational members needed to to initiate change for the total organizaton in the Early Adopters and Interested Users.

Unfortunately, the majority of the professional-development programs focus most of the effort and dollars on trying to get the Not Interested and Reluctant Users to move forward with change. Those programs are not having much impact on the district. The programs with the most impact are stuctured from the opposite viewpoint. They are multistrand programs providing multiple levels of professional development, not a one-size-fits-all approach. Here is how they are stuctured and the types of activites focused on specific user groups:

Early Adopters (20 Percent of Fund Allocation)

- These are the people you use for your pilot projects to determine if a specific application, concept, or tool actually works the way you expect it to work.
- If it works in their classroom, you can release it to all users or install it in the remainder of your classrooms.
- Professional development for this group is more effective when provided as job-embedded professional development, professional-development assistance provided in their classroom.
- The selection mechanisms would be mini grants based on a submission from the teacher.
- The funds allocated for this group are more discretionary in nature.
- These activites are purely site based, not centralized.
- There is litle need to provide incentives for this group of users.

Interested Users (60 Percent of Allocation)

- This is the group where the majority of your money and effort should be focused.
- Provide structured and to-the-point opportunities focused on inter-mediate skill sets.
- Focus on activites that have already demonstrated benefit for student academic acheivement.
- Most districts who have been successful have used job-embedded professional-development delivery, in the classroom, with this group of users.
- These teachers are the group where you will find your future trainers for a Train-the-Trainer process.
- Working in collaboration with others yields a high level of learning efficiency.
- Survey users to determine range of activites required.
- Provide generic, beneficial-for-all, and content-area-specific profesional-development acitivities.
- Provide both site-based and centralized training opportunities.

Reluctant Users (20 Percent of Allocation)

- Provide structured activities that are more awareness and beginning skill sets.
- Provide generic activities, useful to all attendess.
- It appears more effective to deliver profesional development for this group in larger groups, site based or centralized.
- Focus on activities where other teachers within the district have demonstrated improved student academic acheivement.
- Working in collaboration with others yields a high level of learning efficiency.
- Provide both site-based and centralized activities.
- Once members of this group see a trend toward organizational change, incentives help to engage this group in the organizational change.

Not Interested Users (0 Percent of Allocation)

- Attempt to enage this group with reluctant-user activities.
- Without a personal interest to learn and change, there is little benefit from efforts focused on this group.

Within this type of a multistrand professional-development structure, the percentage of members of the organization that makes up the Not

Interested Users will decrease over time to only 1 or 2 percent. Those individuals who are not interested in changing will either retire or move to a different employment opportunity where they will not be required to adopt change.

A bit of a side trip here; we know a lot about how individuals learn. We should be applying student-centered twenty-first-century learning and teaching concepts and processes to how teachers learn these new skills and competencies. Discussions, hands-on projects, and teaching others are the best methods for teachers to learn also. Every teacher has experienced that "teachable moment" when the learner is ready to learn. In the same manner, job-embedded professional development where a learning and teaching coach comes into the classroom when the teacher is ready to learn is the most effective method of professional-development delivery.

To repeat a concept, the primary purpose of a multistrand professional-development program is to motivate and enable 30 percent of the organization members to adopt change. The change we are looking for is that the teacher is using student-centered twenty-first-century learning and teaching concepts and processes with embedded technology for the majority of the student experiences occurring in their classroom.

We are also looking for principals who have the same level of competencies so they can effectively manage the organizational members in their building, ensuring their students experience student-centered twenty-first-century learning and teaching. The focus is back to the center silo, "What/How Students Learn."

PROFESSIONAL-DEVELOPMENT
SCOPE AND SEQUENCE MATRIX

Now that we have established the concept of a multistrand professional-development program, what do we use as a structure for the program? The following table is called a Professional-Development Scope and Sequence Matrix. There are two distinct sets of competencies that virtually all members of the organization need to master. The first is student-centered twenty-first-century learning and teaching concepts and processes and the second is technology literacy. The matrix defines a sequential competency level of mastery for both skill sets aligned with the member position.

The above is a generic version that provides a reasonable overview of the concept. Each district would need to take the concept of the matrix and develop a more detailed description of the competencies the member would need to demonstrate at each level of mastery. The matrix should be broken down into smaller modules and each module has an identifica-

Staff Professional Development
Scope and Sequence Matrix

		Teacher / Media Specialist / Instruct. Specialist	Principal	Administrator	Classified
21st CENTURY LEARNING and TEACHING	MASTER	Advanced Level AND Portfolio of 21st Century L&T Student Experiences Designed By Teacher (Individually or In A Group)	Demonstrate Knowledge of 21st Century L&T Concepts & Practices	Demonstrate Knowledge of District 21st Century L&T Concepts & Policies	Not Applicable
	ADVANCED	Majority of Student Experiences Are Oriented to 21st Century L&T Concepts and Practices			
	INTERMEDIATE	Starting to Use Student Experiences Oriented to 21st Century L&T Concepts and Practices (33%)	Can Assess and Manage L&T Practices Of Their Teachers	Can Assess and Manage L&T Practices Of Principals	
	BASIC	Demonstrate Knowledge of 21st Century L&T Concepts and Practices			
TECHNOLOGY LITERACY / FLUENCY	ADVANCED	Portfolio of Student Experiences Designed By The Staff Member (Individually or In A Group) With Embedded Technology	Demonstrate Basic Computer Skills and Use Personal Productivity Tools	Demonstrate Basic Computer Skills and Use Personal Productivity Tools	Demonstrate Basic Computer Skills and Personal Productivity Tools Equal to Job Description Minimum Requirements
	INTERMEDIATE	Demonstrate Computer Skills and Personal Productivity Tools Equal to Grade Level or Job Description Minimum Requirements	Can Assess Skill Level of Employees They Manage	Can Assess Skill Level of Employees They Manage	
	BASIC	Demonstrate Basic Computer Skills – Troubleshooting - Personal Productivity Tools			

Professional Development opportunities should be offered as a "Blended" learning environment; self-paced individualized, web based, coach with teacher, small group, structured classes. Demonstration of mastery for Basic and certain Intermediate level skill sets should be self-paced tests while other Intermediate, and all Advanced, and Master levels are portfolio based.

tion number (the rationale behind using an ID is explored a little further on). We also need to recognize that the competencies required for a fifth-grade teacher and elementary-school principal are not the same as those required for the science-lab teacher at a high school and the high-school principal.

Those districts that have used this concept to assist their teachers and principals in gaining the desired competencies have also found that the Basic and mid-level Intermediate competencies are best gained through a self-paced process.

Similar to the LOTS-HOTS progression for students, it is quite simple to deliver and assess the Basic skills through a self-directed automated process. As examples: Does the teacher or principal know the elements of student-centered twenty-first-century learning and teaching? Either they know or do not know. Can the teacher create formative assessment tools matched to a student experience? Can the principals assess that the formative assessments are appropriate? Again, either they can or cannot.

Can the teacher create a spreadsheet for data input and design an array that provides analysis of the data? Can the principal recognize a correctly working spreadsheet with array? Either it works or it does not work. Can the teacher complete a specific exercise that demonstrates the ability to design and animate a PowerPoint type of presentation? Again, either it works or it does not work. All of those types of activities can be automated and the teachers can work on them at their own pace. The principal should be capable of recognizing the skill level.

There may be value to creating awareness in a centralized class environment but the real work of your professional-development program for basic skills is now classroom or off-campus based, available at any time, self-directed and self-paced. That is a radically different professional-development environment than what most districts implement. The successful districts also find it very helpful to have some type of gauge/chart that indicates what level of mastery the teacher has achieved for both teacher and management use.

On the other hand, demonstration of the HOTS, where the teacher has used those student-centered twenty-first-century learning and teaching and technology competencies to create a student experience, will require more of a portfolio approach. Additionally, the projects documented in the portfolio should also demonstrate professional collaboration with teachers of the same grade level or content areas. Do your principals have the skills to recognize what they are seeing?

The purpose of the Scope and Sequence Matrix is to clearly articulate the competencies teachers and principals are expected to obtain in order to operate in the student-centered twenty-first-century learning and teaching environment the district is planning to create or has created. The goal is to have every member of the organization functioning in the Intermediate–Advanced range of student-centered twenty-first-century learning and teaching concepts and processes and at the Intermediate range of technology literacy.

The departments of education from all states were required to develop new teacher and principal evaluation systems in order to obtain their NCLB waiver, which in turn makes the state eligible to receive its Title 1 grants from the U.S. Department of Education. Obviously, those evaluations have been aligned to the CCS or new curriculums, reflecting teacher and principal competencies expected by the CCS. Using the Scope and Sequence Matrix concept and enabling teachers to reach the competency goals outlined in the paragraph above, your teachers would meet your state competency requirements.

Once you have the professional-development Scope and Sequence developed, the next step is to realign your current professional-development activities. Every district has some type of professional development going on but it will most likely not be the type of activities most needed by your teachers. There will be early release days, teacher work days, and some professional-development days at the beginning of the school year.

INSTRUCTIONAL DELIVERY PREFERENCES

Everyone has strengths, weaknesses, and preferences based on a number of factors and influences. That implies teachers will have preferences for one type of student-centered learning delivery versus another. Specific student-centered learning delivery methods will resonate with one teacher and not resonate with the one in the classroom next door. The concept that every teacher in a school district should be required to use type "A" versus type "B" student-centered learning activity flies in the face of reality and learning research. A district, or worse, a state department of education stating, "We want all teachers to only use project-based learning" misses the boat. Perhaps a "flipped classroom" environment is the best fit for the teacher and the area of content where they have responsibility for student learning.

There are teachers who can create extremely engaging lectures and perhaps at a curriculum turning point that would work well. However, those teachers would need to mix that instructional delivery method with other styles since a lecture fails to assist the learner in developing HOTS or the 4 Cs of twenty-first-century skills. Additionally, if there is information out there that clearly delineates a specific type of student-centered learning as superior to another type of student-centered learning, it is not readily available. There is little data related to comparison of student-centered learning methodologies, just traditional teacher-centered versus student-centered learning.

We have learner profiling systems as noted in the prior chapter but there are no profiling systems assisting teachers in understanding their areas of strength and weakness regarding their personal approach to instruction. More experienced teachers understand their preferences, and as they delve deeper into the profession they gain comfort with student learning activities that lie outside those preferences. They end up with a large and diverse collection of instructional approaches within their comfort zone, enabling them to flex with the learners in their classroom. Forcing learners to conform to the teacher preferences represents a less effective and efficient culture of learning.

This concept should have a profound impact on your professional-development program. When we talk about developing a Scope and Sequence Matrix for twenty-first-century learning, it should have a list of expected competencies that includes the different student-centered learning instructional delivery methods identified by the district. The professional-development program then has activities that expose and educate each teacher regarding that competency. As teachers work through the multiple delivery methods, they demonstrate their competency. The professional-development program should also provide instruction regarding how teachers align the learner profile with the instructional delivery method. That will deeply tie your professional-development program to your learning culture.

TEACHER AND PRINCIPAL TECHNOLOGY LITERACY

The CCS has quite a few technology-based activities embedded in the expected student experience that imply specific skill sets. If teachers do not have the technology skill sets equal to the technology literacy expected from their students, teachers will not be efficient in facilitating the student experience. Once you have defined student technology literacy, we need to define the associated technology literacy for teachers. The following is part of the English–language arts content for freshman:

Research to Build and Present Knowledge

W.9-10.8 Gather relevant information from multiple authoritative print and digital sources, using advanced searches effectively; assess the usefulness of each source in answering the research question; integrate information into the text selectively to maintain the flow of ideas, avoiding plagiarism and following a standard format for citation.

This writing standard goes particularly well with the CCS Speaking and Listening Standard:

SL.9-10.1. Initiate and participate effectively in a range of collaborative discussions (one-on-one, in groups, and teacher-led) with diverse partners on grade 9-10 topics, texts, and issue, building on others' ideas and expressing their own clearly and persuasively.

As the faculty member managing this student experience you would need to know:

- What is an advanced search? i.e., using Boolean logic searches.
- Which search engine or source best matches the information being researched?
- How do you determine the veracity (authoritativeness) of the sources? Do you know that different search engines use different

weighting factors in the algorithms? Google ranks sources based on how many other places the source is cited but it does not assess the quality of the citation source. Other search engines weigh professional citations from the same field heavier than citations from the general public. Other search engines actually calculate the requested information from public databases.

- How do your students track their activities so you can assess the validity of the process they used to gather their information? Can this be an automatic tracking system?
- Do you know what strategies best enable and control one-to-one or small-group collaborative discussions in your instructional space?
- Do you know how to lead collaborative discussions with your students?
- What resources/tools will your students use to document and present their findings? Do you know how to use those resources and tools so you can facilitate the process?

How many of your teachers have technology literacy that could support this activity? A major initiative for all districts is to conduct an actual assessment of their teachers and principals regarding student-centered twenty-first-century learning and teaching concepts and processes and technology literacy. Then the professional-development program will need to address the specific needs of teachers and principals. As stated at the beginning of the chapter, school districts are in the same position as corporate America. You will need to retrain your employees to match the needs of your organization.

You will also experience the same issue we discussed with students. What happens when your new member of the teaching or administrative staff comes from another school district that has been less successful in enabling teachers to gain the competencies they need?

As noted in the section on student technology literacy, there is a need to have the student technology competencies aligned with the appropriate grade-level requirements of the CCS. Once you have student literacy defined, then your district can define the technology competency required for the teacher or principal appropriate for their grade level. Most of the discussions held along these lines group teachers along the lines of PreK–2, 3–5, 6–8, and high-school competencies.

ACCOUNTABILITY

The next question has an extremely wide range of responses dependent upon what part of the country you live in and how your state department of education developed their new teacher- and principal-evaluation systems. Reflecting that the CCS requires a student-centered twenty-first-century learning and teaching environment, how will you make your teachers and principals accountable for gaining the required competencies? How will you create a quality management process for monitoring the quality of student experiences?

This Creating a Culture of Learning Plan with Roadmap has just become much more complex and full of politically charged energy. However, making teachers and principals accountable for competencies reflecting the CCS-driven, student-centered, twenty-first-century learning and teaching is a pivot point.

As mentioned in the overview, this plan must address all silos. If you leave the issue of teacher and principal accountability untouched and do not develop a strategy for how your district will move forward, this plan will have little impact on student achievement. Your Early Adopters will move to a student-centered learning environment but the district will not achieve the 30 percent "buy-in" required to change the entire organization.

You will end up with an environment where "Some of the Students, Most of the Time" (a minority) will experience student-centered learning environments. It will show up in your lack of improvement in student academic achievement. That is not very fair to your students. It is a sensitive issue but it must be addressed.

However, we do not want the conversation to revolve around the negative connotations of "accountability." Corporate America has found that members of their organization do not deliver quality efforts because leadership demands, dictates, mandates, or even provides incentives, especially in twenty-first-century knowledge businesses. The members must actively choose to act in a manner that results in quality efforts. It is the leadership's responsibility to create a culture of support, enabling the members of the organization to obtain the skills they need and voluntarily using those skills to meet the quality expectations of the organization. Yes, all members of an organization need to be accountable for their activities, but the opposite side is that the organization must create a culture of support focused on quality. How do we help to make things go right?

The new teacher- and principal-evaluation systems provide the accountability. They will be held accountable for development of their competency regarding student-centered twenty-first-century learning and teaching concepts and processes, which will include embedded technology. The districts will be rated by the state department and those results will be published.

There is an interesting aspect of a state-generated evaluation system that expects to drive change. On one hand it outlines expectations that will be measured, and on the other it does not provide a plan or process explaining how the users will gain the skills required to meet those expectations. The users see what they are expected to be capable of doing but cannot see when, where, or how they will obtain the skills needed. The words *fear, uncertainty,* and *doubt* come to mind; let's call it the FUD Factor. Every initiative or project will have a period of time where the FUD (fear, uncertainty, and doubt) Factor seems to be in control. We need to minimize the FUD Factor.

We need to go back to the concept of the professional-development Scope and Sequence Matrix from earlier in this chapter. The evaluation systems are essentially aligned with the CCS, which means aligned with student-centered twenty-first-century learning and teaching concepts and processes with embedded technology. In your district, you flesh out the details of what skills and knowledge belong in each level of the professional-development Scope and Sequence Matrix aligned with the CCS.

You assess your teachers and principals to determine where in the sequence their skills are aligned. You then use the multistrand professional-development-program concept to assist the users to develop their skill sets to a level that meets expectations. We have addressed the aspects of uncertainty and doubt. We know exactly what skills the teachers and principals need and we know the sequence of how they will obtain them. We address the issue of fear by implementing a professional-development process focused on a minimum of 30 percent of the members moving to adopt change. That would be creating a culture of support focused on quality.

There is another aspect to this issue that relates back to the discussion of formative assessment in the prior chapter. Chapter 3 pointed out the disconnect between student summative assessments and teachers having data in a manner that enables timely correction of student knowledge gaps. We need to think about teacher and principal accountability from the same viewpoint.

Using an annual evaluation to determine if teachers or principals are meeting the goals of the district creates the same type of time disconnect. Teachers and principals need timely data regarding their performance. If we wait until the annual assessment, there is little chance we can effectively correct the problem. Accountability is not about "Blame and Shame" but about providing assistance when it is needed.

One last item before we leave teacher accountability. There is a misconception regarding how easy or hard it will be to create a culture of support. It does not automatically follow that it will be easier in states with right-to-work statutes versus being harder in states with collective bargaining statutes. It can land almost anywhere regardless of which category your state is in. It has more to do with the long-standing relationship between the executive leadership of the district and the teachers, or the association representing the teachers.

If that relationship has been a collaborative working relationship, striving to focus on the success of students, a pathway that addresses the issues surrounding teacher accountability can be found. If the relationship is more adversarial, focusing on what the contract does and does not allow, or executive leadership issues mandates without collaborating with teachers, it is much harder. Perhaps in those situations, starting the conversation from the viewpoint of what the students need based on the CCS and how that affects teachers and principals can redirect the efforts to find a pathway to address accountability issues. To reemphasize a prior point, leaving this silo of professional development incomplete will reduce the chance that this plan has a real impact on student achievement to a one out of two shot or less.

INCENTIVES

Creating a culture of support includes understanding what your organizational members consider an incentive. This is another area that is hard to nail down in that the range of what members of an educational organization consider an incentive is again all over the place. Some readers may respond that learning new competencies is required for members to perform their jobs; why should the district provide an incentive for members to do their jobs? We will refer back to the general trend of contemporary organization-management research.

Creating a culture of support involves finding those things that motivate the members of the organization to voluntarily meet the goals of the organization, while managing themselves on a daily basis. The point is that the organization uses incentives to be explicit about encouraging the type of behavior they want the members to exhibit.

Providing an incentive for the Early Adopters is typically fairly straightforward. They want some training and the supporting technology and for the district to get out of their way. They are already motivated and have no issues with simply forging forward. The incentive is typically giving them the hardware and software they request. You want to take advantage of that attitude, but they need to provide the district with something in return.

The district needs to be able to determine if what the Early Adopter attempts as a pilot project actually impacts student achievement in a positive manner. The pilot project should include some type of mutually agreeable method that compares students in the pilot project to students who do not participate in the pilot project or comparison of academic achievement from last year to this year. It also needs to be much more granular, more detailed on a more regular basis, than a simple comparison test outcome. This model of comparative analysis should be part and parcel of every pilot project.

The Interested Users represent another group of members who are interested in advancing their competencies without expecting special incentives, but not at the breakneck speed of the Early Adopters. For most of them, the incentive is to see the academic achievement of their students improve. They are interested in being made aware of successful models of student-centered twenty-first-century learning and teaching and how it will apply to the academic rigor of the CCS.

Once they are convinced of the connection, they are interested in learning how to deliver learning through that model. This is why the pilot projects must have a comparative analysis data function embedded in the project. The demonstrations and sharing of outcomes can occur during the normal professional development schedule (teacher work days, early release, etc.). That group of members simply wants a structured approach to how members are trained and equipped to facilitate the twenty-first-century learning environment.

That means they have been: released from the classroom to receive training (district funds substitutes); their classroom has been provided with the technology that enables the student experience; and there is job-embedded assistance when they try their first student experience. The higher-level incentive is improved student academic achievement, but the down-to-earth incentive is for the district to make it easy to learn and implement the new model of learning. If there are friction points that cause delay or extra effort, they will consider the exercise a failure and it will be much harder to encourage them to change in the future.

It is important to point out that to the organization leaders that it will take two to three years to reach that 30 percent level that is so critical for change to occur. It does not happen quickly—be patient.

Now we come to the remainder of the members of the organization. If you have the 30 percent moving forward, the incentive is not what they can get from the organization but what they need to do to keep up with their peers. Very few people want to be considered inadequate in their chosen profession.

If you understand this section correctly, when you structure your professional-development process correctly, you are creating a culture of support. The incentives noted above are not financial in nature. Granted, if you expect members of the organization to be trained during days that are not covered by their employment contract, then you will need to pay a stipend. However, the things most people consider incentives are the things you should be doing to create your district's culture of support.

TEACHER AND PRINCIPAL EFFICACY

Today's paper- and digital-based teacher documentation and reporting processes burden faculty members with many points of friction, creating a discouraging impact on their efficacy. If teachers think today's classroom management is burdensome, it is simple when compared to a true student-centered learning environment where the academic achievement of each student is tracked on an almost daily basis and the teacher analyzes and facilitates the next step for that student. We cannot manage a student-centered twenty-first-century learning and teaching environment without automating all classroom management functions and quite a few of the teacher reporting requirements.

School districts need to make a concerted effort to automate any function performed by teachers that an algorithm can complete. Removal of these friction points is also necessary to enable teachers to manage a student-centered learning environment. It is impossible to manage that environment, taking into account each student's learning style and readiness, without using technology as the management tool. It is also important to understand that all of these tools need to be web-browser-based applications, not the older-style client-server.

We will list a number of systems; some are traditional systems and others are suggested by the new student experience indicated in the CCS. The systems are listed separately but a number of vendors have developed applications that merge a number of these systems into the same application. Each vendor touts their unique configuration as superior but what really matters is how easy it is for teachers to use, and how easy it is for the district to grab data from that application. These are not exhaustive descriptions, just generic overviews that indicate the function for the category of system listed. In one way or another, the district needs:

- *Student Information System (SIS)*—This is the main tool used for administrative management of students. In a collapsed-administration-system concept, it is the primary database that all other systems use, eliminating double entry of students and maintaining more than one database.
- *Gradebook*—This application handles records associated with student examinations, assessments, marks, grades, and academic progress.
- *Learning Management System (LMS)*—The LMS provides teachers with the curriculum alignment, curriculum calendar/pacing guideline, and the ability to post teacher-designed student experiences (included associated content, connections, resources) with related formative assessments aligned to the curriculum. The system should also allow the user to post videos or web-based lessons, providing

direction to other teachers as to how to use the technology associated with the associated student experience. This is where the vision
rubric should be used by the teacher to align the classroom activity
with the overall vision for learning and teaching. The system should
also enable teachers to categorize the type of instructional delivery
method(s) utilized as part of the student experience.

- *eAssessment System*—This is a collection of test items teachers can use
  for online examinations and assessments that are not yet aligned to
  a student experience. The system also grades the student response.
  While it is much easier to assess LOTS through multiple choice,
  progress is being made in developing grading methods that measure
  HOTS from typed answers.

- *Social-Media Interface to LMS*—It has been demonstrated that students
  prefer using their standard social-media methods of communicating
  with their teachers and instructional peers (e-mail, Facebook, Twitter). However, there are legal ramifications and control of appropriate content issues associated with students using their personal
  accounts in schools. The solution for school districts is to provide
  a social-media-*like* implementation of those applications within the
  boundaries of the school campuses and operations and their students
  use those applications for school-associated activities.

- *Formative Assessment Data*—This is the formative assessment data
  attached to each student experience used for real-time analysis of
  what the student did or did not learn, determining what experience
  should occur tomorrow. Whether this data should be part of the
  gradebook, providing more granular information as to the academic
  progress of each student, is a valid question. Each district will answer the question differently.

- *Student Data Dashboard*—As noted in prior sections, real-time access
  to formative assessment data is crucial to a student-centered learning
  environment. However, not all data is located in the SIS and getting
  to the information required by teachers to perform their Instructional
  Analysis can be quite tedious. The districts will need to find or develop a web-browser-based access to ALL student information that is
  very simple and straightforward for teachers to use. I am not talking
  about building a data warehouse but rather new technology, a web
  tool called ORM. ORM gathers data from various sources you point
  it to in real time and allows you to run queries about that data. For
  teachers, they can run a predefined query in their web browser and
  up comes a data dashboard indicating the learning status of each
  student, enabling teachers to plan tomorrow's activities.

These systems also provide the means for principals to monitor teacher activities on a more real-time basis. It is not fair to the students for the principal to find out from the annual student assessment that there is an area of content where the teacher is struggling. A realistic approach to student-centered learning requires review of the data and an assessment of when and where assistance is needed. The systems are electronic and do not require the principal to physically relocate to the classroom.

It does not remove the formal evaluation process but enables the principal a quick review process of teacher activity. There is a need of transparency for the process; that the teacher is notified of the electronic review and perhaps a copy of the assessment provided with the notice. Chapter 5 provides a more detailed overview of how this process would work under the quality management section.

The issue to be addressed with these systems is how to make management of a student-centered twenty-first-century learning and teaching environment less of a burden. We want teachers to facilitate learning rather than constantly reporting on learning. The data should speak for itself.

Assessment Questions Associated with the "Professional Development" Silo:

- Does the district have a multistrand approach to professional development?
- If not, how would you describe its professional-development approach?
- Is professional development delivered only in central locations?
- Is professional development delivered at the building level?
- Does the district provide job embedded professional development?
- Has the district developed a professional-development Scope and Sequence?
- Has that Scope and Sequence been shared with the members of the organization?
- Does it contain student-centered twenty-first-century learning and teaching concepts and processes?
- To what level of detail? (Has the district defined student-centered twenty-first-century learning and teaching literacy?)
- Does it contain teacher and principal technology literacy expectations?
- To what level of detail? (Has the district defined twenty-first-century technology literacy?)
- Are teachers and principals held accountable to gain competencies in both of those areas?
- If so, how?

- Does the district provide incentives to members for gaining those competencies?
- If so, how?
- Does the district have online (web-browser-based) applications—note which product—for:
  - Student Information System
  - Gradebook
  - Learning Management System
  - eAssessment System
  - Social-Media Interface for LMS
  - Formative Assessment Data
  - Student Data Dashboard

Chapter 5

Policies and Processes

As mentioned in the introduction, most student-centered twenty-first-century learning and teaching demonstration projects have a unique leadership structure that enables the project to succeed, but once that leader departs, the project struggles. When that happens, it indicates the district did not address changes of policies and processes required to support the demonstration environment. The changes required to align with the best practices as described in this chapter will enable the district to make all of the 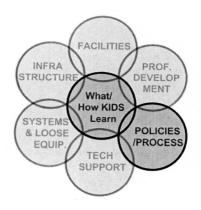 changes sustainable. Again, some of these best practices are a representations of successful concepts from other districts and concepts that I have expanded. This chapter is focused on how you create a culture of learning in your district.

ORGANIZATIONAL STRUCTURE

The organizational structure of an educational entity implies many things about the culture and politics of that organization. All aspects of the student-centered twenty-first-century learning and teaching environment in a school district, including the technical support department, belong

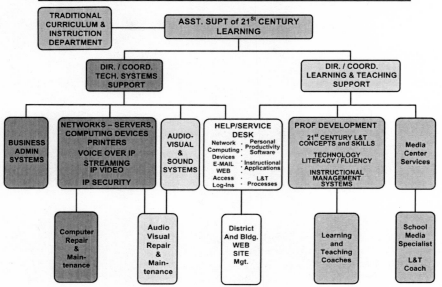

IDEAL STRUCTURE FOR 21st CENTURY L&T With TECHNOLOGY SUPPORT

underneath the instructional leadership of the district. This is contrary to the operations within most school districts in the United States.

The reader may have noted that we are not using the term "IT department" but rather "technical support." That concept will be explored more in depth in the next chapter. In the meantime, here is the rationale behind the belief that technical support should be under curriculum and instruction based on observations in multiple school districts.

All technology hardware and software purchases should be driven by and anchored to the student experience: "What/How They Learn." Experience from a multitude of district-wide technology programs indicate that more than 90 percent of the total technology expenditures over a ten-year period of time are made for instructional purposes. So the primary client of the technical support department is the curriculum and instruction department. Placing tech support in a separate arm of the organization places artificial barriers between the user (curriculum and instruction, their teachers, and the students) and the service provider (technical support).

Those barriers simply make the process of student-centered twenty-first-century learning and teaching more difficult, impacting the efficiency of the organization. Corporate America learned a long time ago that when a company is relying upon a subcontractor for more than 50 percent of the components or services making up their business, they must acquire the subcontractor or there is a high risk of failure when conditions change in the subcontractor. Pulling the subcontractor into the fold assures a continued access to the primary products and services they need to succeed in the marketplace. In a similar manner, the majority of tech-support-department services and expenditures are related to instruction; therefore, tech support needs to be part of the curriculum and instructional department.

This does not eliminate nor diminish the need of technical support to manage and enable the back office administrative systems required to conduct the business of a school district.

We also need to recognize that one of the reasons why school districts have placed technology in a separate silo is that no one really understands what tech support does. The organization only understands when things are not working correctly. The ideal organizational diagram has many implications and chapter 6 will delve into the actual workings of what a technical support department should look like.

An observation for the smaller school districts: regardless of your size, someone in your organization will be responsible for all of the activities in the diagram. Typically, that means an individual is fulfilling more than one function, wearing many hats. Larger districts may have an entire staff fulfilling one function.

KEEPER OF THE PLAN

If student-centered twenty-first-century learning and teaching with technology inclusion is to be effective, most schools with a successful program evolve to a different level of coordination from the central administrative office to the campus level. It becomes more important for a key district-level person to become the keeper of the Creating a Culture of Learning Plan with Roadmap, supervising the implementation and being responsible for operational and user support. It is their responsibility to make sure the instructional learning that occurs is well articulated, shared, understood, and acted upon from a systems approach. They become the main communication conduit through which the superintendent and cabinet can judge the progress of the staff.

That *Keeper of the Plan* should be located somewhere within the instructional side of the structure. It helps for that person to be executive level, ensuring he or she has sufficient political weight that all members of the organization understand that this is important to the district. This person will be one of the leaders in the district regarding how students learn, so a strong instructional background and understanding of the concepts and processes of student-centered twenty-first-century learning is needed for this position.

It is also important that the person has a high level of technology literacy. Direct knowledge and understanding of the technology is not needed, but the person should have high-level competencies regarding how technology supports student-centered twenty-first-century learning and teaching. Regardless of the size of your school district, this is a very important position and must have a person with the correct skill sets. If there are no qualified people within the district, perhaps the district needs to create a new position underneath the head of curriculum and recruit someone to that position from the outside. Similar to the comments regarding smaller and larger school districts, this person may need to wear more than one hat.

COMMUNICATION CHANNELS AND ROLES

One of the major tasks this person will fill is the creation of communications channels between all departments within the organization and to and from building-level personnel. Some districts have made this a separate set of committees and others have included the functions in existing committees (typically curriculum committees). I must admit a preference for the latter but regardless, each district needs communications across all departments.

If you work in a school district you will find the following a realistic scenario. The Title 1 folks apply for a special grant that provides computers for PreK–3 classrooms running an application for reading literacy. No one else in the district knows about the application. The district is successful with their application and here come the computers and software.

Oh wait! No one told the facilities department that there are one hundred new computers coming in and they need electrical power in the older classrooms. No one told the technical support group that they need to install one hundred new data ports in the older classrooms. While it is great that the Title 1 folks were successful, their success is totally disruptive to two other departments that did not allocate funds or expect to lose manpower capacity to that project. That Title 1 project has now taken resources that were supposed to be applied to some other project those departments had planned to accomplish this year. That is what we call inefficiency.

The following diagram provides an overview of observed best practices related to what I call the "Formal Communication Channels/Roles." The primary goal of a formal communication structure is to ensure the correct people are involved and aware of all learning and technology initiatives that may impact their specific areas of interest. The intent of the communication structure is to enable consistent bidirectional communication

FORMAL COMMUNICATION CHANNELS / ROLES

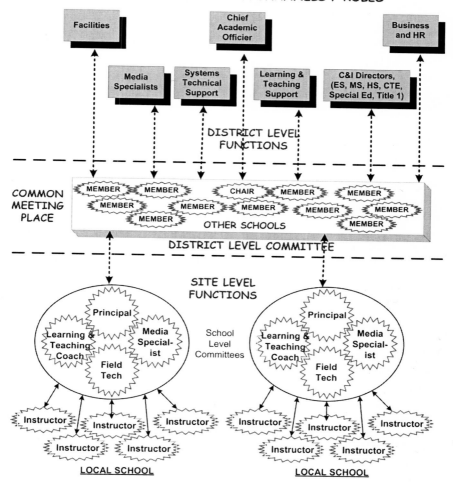

horizontally across district-level departments, and vertically from the district level to the school level, and from the school level to the classroom (and vice versa).

The common meeting point for all information flow is the required attendance by key personnel at a formal and scheduled monthly meeting. Rather than create a separate or new committee, it works best to meld these functions into existing committees, preferably curriculum oriented since the goal is to enhance communications between all departments and school regarding student-centered twenty-first-century learning and teaching. The members of this district-level committee are:

- Either the chief academic officer or one of the executive directors/ coordinator for systems technical support or learning and teaching support who answers to the chief academic officer of the district is the chair of the district committee. As the manager of this process, this person has the responsibility and authority to ensure the participation of all district departments and campus sites.
- A representative from every major department at the district level who would be responsible for communications from their respective district department to the district committee and from the committee to the department.
- If a curriculum-oriented committee does not exist at each school, that school should form its own school steering committee. This committee is responsible for communicating district committee information to the classroom and classroom information to the district committee. A representative from the individual school steering committee is responsible for communications from his or her campus to the district committee and from the district committee to his or her campus.
- In larger districts, there may be the need to create a level of technology committees between the district and building levels dependent upon the number of schools.

This formal communication structure has a tremendous impact on the efficiency of learning and teaching initiatives, communication, and technology implementation. Each department should be reporting to the group regarding grant applications and initiatives being planned and the current status. The other departments can ask questions that should start their departmental planning processes. In larger school districts this meeting occurs on a monthly basis. Smaller districts can make it work with meetings every other month and then more often as major initiatives occur.

There are formal meeting minutes with a set agenda separated into old and new business. Old business is where a grant or initiative has been reported at a prior meeting and this is an update of its status. It should also trigger ongoing discussion with the other departments affected by the grant or initiative. The grant or initiative stays on the agenda until it has been completed. These formal minutes are very important in that any district will have more things happening than any one person can remember.

Through this communication method we are assured that when a grant is awarded or an initiative comes up from a school site, or a district-wide initiative is planned from the district level, all of the key areas impacted by those initiatives are gathered in one place at one time for the purposes of:

- Discussion regarding merits of initiative
- Ensuring areas impacted by an initiative are considered
- Communication and coordination in the planning of an initiative, alerting other departments
- Communication and coordination of the initiative implementation

It should be noted that the formal communication channel to the typical classroom teacher occurs at the local campus level through the school-level committee. The local school member of the district committee not only receives information from the district committee for dissemination but is also the liaison from the district committee down to the building committee. In addition, that person is also the liaison from the school-level committee back up to the district committee.

As indicated in the diagram, there should be a bidirectional flow of information. It is unfortunate that the district level has outlined how things will happen in the classroom only to find out that the teachers' response is, "Oh no, that doesn't work very well, we do it this way." The district-level personnel have no real idea what teachers do or do not do in the classroom. There must be a communication channel from the classroom back up to the district level.

These committees are an excellent channel for sharing the district Creating a Culture of Learning Plan and Roadmap. In addition to the district committee member from the school being trained regarding the plan and roadmap, you also train the principals, perhaps separately from the district-committee-education process. Now you have a minimum of two people who understand the district's Creating a Culture of Learning Plan with Roadmap at each school.

The local school committee functions as the first line of alignment of classroom student activities and the overall goals of the organization. Once the executive level (extended cabinet) has understood and bought into the concepts of the plan and roadmap the school committee starts the process of disseminating information about the plan and roadmap on its campus.

The agenda and sequence of information with support documentation should be generated by the curriculum and instruction department so all school committees are delivering the same message. It is this committee's responsibility to disseminate the district's Learning and Teaching Roadmap concepts, starting with the Mission for Twenty-First-Century Learning and Teaching, to all teachers in its building.

The school committee is also the campus-level agent that receives grant requests from the Early Adopters and Interested Users. It makes sure that the pilot project grants meet the criteria of the district before they are approved at the local level or channeled upstream to the district committee. When the grant reaches the district committee, deemed appropriate, and funded, the other departments are aware of the initiative and can coordinate their work force to assist the pilot project. If the pilot project has positive results, perhaps it moves out to all similar grade level or content areas in the District.

The school committee is also the campus-level group that provides the first line of assurance that all hardware and software purchase requests from the school meet the hardware and software adoption requirements as outlined in the next section.

HARDWARE AND SOFTWARE ADOPTION PROCESSES

Every district needs to have formal hardware and software adoption processes that are centrally driven and enforced at the local level. The lack of these processes will have an impact on the efficiency of technology implementation at the local level and tremendous impact on the ability of the technical support department to support the hardware and software. The following diagram provides a "best practice" as observed for a number of educational organizations across the United States.

Please note that it is a bidirectional process that enables the district level to provide direction to the local site and the local site to provide feedback to the district level regarding what applications and hardware do and do not work, suggesting revisions.

District Level

Within each content area and grade level, an adoption committee chaired by the respective content or grade-level leader reviews the software available that addresses specific aspects of the new curriculum adopted from the CCS. Where there are multiple applications available for the same subject matter, the committee will select a maximum of two software applications that the district will support. That list of software is published on the district website and reviewed on an annual basis.

With regard to hardware components, the district committee forms a subcommittee that establishes a set of standards for all computing devices and AV instructional support systems. The hardware should represent a range of products that reflect the level of technology required to run the application of technology skill sets of the user. That list is published on the district website and reviewed on an annual basis.

SOFTWARE ADOPTION PROCESS

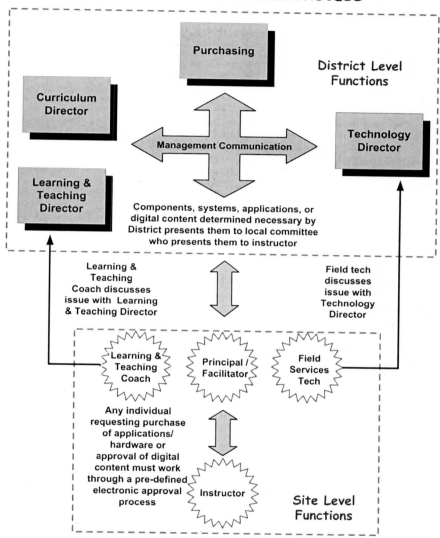

Campus Level

Purchases for software or hardware which are not part of the published list are not allowed by the purchasing department. To accommodate pilot projects and individuals who wish to explore newer and different technologies which may be more efficient than the items on the current list, there is an approval process the individual must work through:

- The proposer will first document the specific area of the curriculum that the software or hardware addresses.
- The proposer will document how he or she plans to use the software or hardware in their instructional process and the expected impact on student learning.
- The local school committee reviews the application for a variation and sponsors the application up their respective chains of command.
  - The learning and teaching coach associated with the local site discusses the application with peers and content-area managers.
  - The technician associated with the local site processes the application with regard to compatibility with current computing operating systems and networking model.
- Subsequent to the instructional validity and hardware compatibility reviews, the application is either recommended for adoption, recommended for revisions, or recommended as not viable at this time.
- The primary function of purchasing within this structure is to enforce the standards established by curriculum and instruction, learning and teaching support, and technology systems support.

QUALITY MANAGEMENT

The entrepreneur business author Michael E. Gerber makes a very astute observation in his book, *The E-Myth Revisited*:[1] "You cannot manage people because people are irrational; however you can manage processes." He is not suggesting that organizations should not create a culture of care and support but rather that you cannot manage people from that viewpoint. We can only manage people based on the how they adhere to the processes we expect them to use as they execute their responsibilities.

Within the framework of a student-centered twenty-first-century learning and teaching environment, it comes down to the student experience. Does the student experience meet the expectations of the organization? Everything should be viewed through the lens of the student experience.

What are those expectations? We need to circle back to the beginning of chapter 3 and the concept of establishing a common Mission for Twenty-First-Century Learning and Teaching that permeates the entire organization from executive level to classroom level. The outcome of that process is the development of a simple teacher rubric applied to all student experiences occurring in their classrooms.

Based on that rubric, the teachers understand the expectations, the principal understands the expectations. The teacher rubric functions as the tool used to align teacher activities to organizational goals and part of the principal's bi-monthly (once every two weeks) quality monitoring process. It would also be used as part of the quality-monitoring process for those who monitor the principals.

Quality monitoring is not a tool used for "Blame and Shame," creating a punitive culture for those who do not measure up. It is a tool that helps to create a culture of support where someone is responsible to review the teacher activities so timely assistance can be provided when needed. The same is applied to the next level up. The administrator responsible for quality monitoring of principals needs timely information to support the principals and teachers under that principal.

Before we go into detail of how that occurs, we need to take a short side trip. Most of the readers may understand how TQM, started by the statistician W. Edwards Deming, completely changed the auto-manufacturing business in Japan, enabling the Japanese to gain a major share of the U.S. auto market. It took a while, but domestic manufacturers also adopted the concept. When most readers think about TQM, they associate it with manufacturing, places that make things. That is where it started, but it has expanded into every conceivable area of business, not just manufacturing. There are multiple authors of methods for how you apply TQM concepts to various industries and offer "certificates" for individuals who have completed training on their particular method. There are so many different ways to do TQM that those certification processes have become a multibillion-dollar-a-year industry unto themselves.

As related to the purposes of creating a student-centered culture of learning, understanding the basic concept of TQM will suffice.

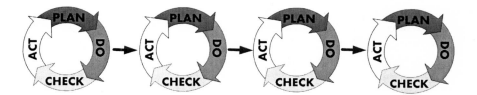

TOTAL QUALITY MANAGEMENT
Repeated Activities - Teacher Rubric

Deming came up with the concept that improvement in the quality of design, product quality, testing, and sales is achieved by a continual process of Plan, Do, Check, and Act. The diagram indicates that it is a continual process, one step feeding the next step, feeding the next step, feeding the next step, and so on. You cannot reach quality for all functions in your organization doing a once-a-year evaluation (student or teacher). It must be a continual cycle, always churning.

Does the diagram remind you of anything we discussed on a prior occasion? It should—the diagram intentionally copies the shapes and colors of the "Data-Driven Student Learning" model used in chapter 3. None of the data-driven student learning literature explicitly indicates that the originators of the concept used the Deming model but the data-driven student learning process is a TQM process adapted to the educational environment:

This is a process that occurs in the classroom almost on a daily basis. So, back to how we execute this type of TQM in a K–12 educational environment. First, we will go back to the teacher rubric created from the district mission for learning and teaching. Let's review the one from chapter 3.

Is your planned student experience:
- Engaging?
- Focusing on twenty-first-century skills?
- Applying grade-level core knowledge?

Using the LMS, it should be straightforward for the teachers to find student experiences aligned to the curriculum which meet those criteria. (Remember, for most teachers, not the Early Adopters, the LMS has a collection of student experiences already posted, even videos of how to use any technology embedded in the student experience.) The student experience should also have a set of formative assessments attached. Once the students have completed the activity, the students take the assessment.

The teacher uses the student data dashboard (chapter 4) to review the outcomes from the activity and determines the next step for individuals or the group. This is a process the teacher continually goes through for the entire instructional year.

In a similar manner, on a regular basis the principal pulls up the student dashboard, which has a teacher module that lists the number of student-centered activities used by the teacher. (As suggested in the last chapter, your LMS needs to allow classifying the student experience and the district would need to create and define that list of classifications.) The principal also opens up the student data dashboard to look at the class outcomes to assess the academic progress. The principal also looks at the teacher progress from their professional-development Scope and Sequence Matrix.

How often should the principal be expected to make this type of an assessment of each teacher's activities? The question should be: how often should the principal assess the teacher's activities to ensure students are meeting the organization's academic expectations? It is about the students; are they receiving what the district expects them to receive? It's not about the teacher. Also remember this is an electronic review. A school district would start with once every two weeks and once everyone is in the rhythm of the process, adjust accordingly.

Based on the assessments, the principal may need to talk to a teacher about what is happening in their classrooms and perhaps assign resources to assist the teachers with specific areas where their students are not reaching academic expectations. The process should focus on discovering substandard activities close to the time they occur and providing timely assistance to correct and improve what students are receiving.

At the next level, the supervisor of the principal would be checking electronically to assess whether the principal is doing assessments on the expected schedule basis. That supervisor would also be able to pull up a student data dashboard on the school as a whole, which should reflect the teacher and principal activities. Once a month would be appropriate. In the same manner, the supervisor may need to talk to the principal regarding the substandard activities occurring in their building and assign resources to assist where needed.

This is a TQM type of process that has defined explicit expectations and metrics (things we use to measure conformation to a process), which can be used to assess if the individual member activities align with the organization's goals. The teacher uses it on a daily basis, the principal uses it on a biweekly basis, and the principal's supervisor uses it once a month. Not only is it straightforward and easy to use, it focuses on the primary goal of the organization, student achievement.

The importance of this TQM process cannot be overemphasized. When the organization is addressing academic performance problems when they occur, your student achievement moves to a whole different level. When coupled with student-centered instructional delivery methodologies, it becomes even more effective.

Funding

Funding issues are as hard to resolve as teacher and principal accountability. Even in a good economic climate, there is not a sufficient amount of revenue to meet all of the needs of the typical school district. Deferred maintenance and similar categories are typically underfunded. It always ends up that the district must prioritize their needs.

In the current economic climate of reduced allocations, it becomes even harder. Funding for student-centered twenty-first-century learning and teaching typically will require a combination of reprioritization, realignment, and reallocation of available revenue at best. There are a number of school districts where cuts have been so severe that there is no flexibility at all.

A concern regarding the small school districts is that they have absolutely no flexibility to reprioritize, realign, or reallocate funds. It may take external assistance at the state level to help those districts in the initial stages of developing a student-centered learning culture.

When we talk about funding mechanisms for operating and capital budgets for schools, there is no limit to the variety of methods used across the United States. It ranges from total local funding mechanisms to primarily state funding with some local funding and all kinds of combinations in between. Additionally, each state has its own set of names for budget categories and they are not similar to the adjacent states.

There are federal revenue sources added to the mix. There are strict guidelines of where those dollars can be used but we need to know how much is available and for what purposes. As an example: if there are funds available for a reading program associated with the PreK through third-grade classrooms, realigning those expenditures for web-browser-based devices rather than full-blown desktop computers will put more student devices in those classrooms using federal money instead of district money.

Funding is also impacted by governance that ranges from small local school districts to large county school districts and again, everything in between. We have already visited the fact that there are approximately 13,600 public school districts in the United States. Over half of those districts have one thousand or fewer students. What you may not know is that the top two hundred systems in size, starting at twenty-five thousand students, represent only 1.6 percent of all school districts, yet they educate 35 percent of all students in the United States.[2]

The larger school districts simply have a larger budget and more employees. Even a small percentage of a shift in their allocation or reprioritization or redefinition of job descriptions can have a big impact on the success of a Learning and Teaching Roadmap.

The small school districts do not have that luxury. Shifting priorities represent a larger percentage of their budget, making it that much more difficult. On top of these variances in size, there are tremendous differences in cultural and political environments between each school district in the country.

Another hindrance to planning is school districts that do not track their instructional and technology expenditures in separate categories. They have no real method for determining how much they have expended from a historical basis; therefore, they cannot project what is available for future years. Some actually provide the funds to the local building and the principal has control of where the money is spent.

All of this is to simply state that it is extremely hard to talk about funding in a competent manner. Therefore, we will keep the conversation at a high level and the reader will need to adapt the concepts to their local mechanisms and terms.

In general, it would be safe to divide schools' budgets into operating and capital budget categories. To make sure we are on the same page: "operating" budgets mean all annual expenditures required to keep the doors open and pay all employees. "Capital" budgets are those used for purchase of land, construction, renovation, deferred maintenance (replace a roof system), and purchase of equipment with at least a five-year life cycle. Most of our discussion will revolve around the operating budget.

Moving your district to a student-centered twenty-first-century learning and teaching environment will have a profound impact on your operating budget. For some districts it will be a redefinition and refocusing of existing allocations and for others it will be a really hard reprioritization to determine which categories receive funding and which ones do not.

Changing the operating budget can be a slow process of shifting priorities from one set of categories to another, easily requiring five years to complete the process. Regardless of how your system operates, the following are basic operating budget categories your district will need to review and reallocate based on the outcomes of your Learning and Teaching Roadmap:

- Curriculum and instruction management systems and applications
- Curriculum and instruction student applications
- Curriculum and instruction grants for special projects
- Textbooks
- Allocations for content specialists*
- Allocations for classroom support specialists (whatever their title may be)*
- Allocations for professional development
- Title 1 allocations
- Title 1 special grants
- Perkins allocations
- Annual computing device refresh funds (replacing existing computing devices)

- Capital expenditures for computing devices (purchasing new computing devices)
- Capital expenditures for servers and storage systems
- Capital expenditures for network upgrades and improvements (hardwired and wireless)
- Capital expenditures for technical support systems (service desk, BYOD management)
- Capital expenditures for classroom AV devices and systems

* Larger districts may have personnel whose primary function is to assist the classroom teacher. When you review the CCS, you may recognize that the expectation is interdisciplinary learning. The concept of content specialists is not reflected in the CCS. Perhaps all of these specialists should become student-centered twenty-first-century learning and teaching coaches.

If you are one of the fortunate school districts with capital budget fund sources and are currently implementing a construction program, you have an excellent opportunity to use those projects as a pivot point to reorient toward a student-centered twenty-first-century learning and teaching culture. The good news is that you have money for purchasing technology and furniture for twenty-first-century learning. The bad news is that the capital budget expenditure needs to be supported by an associated operating budget expenditure.

Experience indicates that in order to ensure that teachers use the capability of the technology you installed in their new classrooms, you will need operating budget expenditures equal to 10 percent of the capital budget expenditures. Those expenditures are targeted directly toward the teachers and principals of the new facilities in preparation for and when they come online. How does that work into your current operating budget?

Additionally, most districts must resolve the long-term/short-term expenditure problem. Computing devices have a life cycle of four or five years at best. There are some basic problems with using twenty-year bond funds to purchase a device that lasts only five years. Different states have resolved this in different ways and other states have not addressed the issue at all.

FUNDING SHIFT ENABLING
COMPUTING DEVICE FOR EVERY STUDENT

There is a major shift coming toward all school districts. That shift is the transition away from printed textbooks toward digital content. We have noted how textbook publishers are completely missing the digital transition. Quite a bit of that view is driven by Clayton Christensen and his book *The Innovators Dilemma*.[3] Christensen wondered why big companies fail; the company he was in charge of failed.

He realized that successful companies are trained by the MBAs from the nation's high-end schools of business to focus on what he calls sustaining innovations. Those are innovations that occur at the more profitable, high end of the market. The innovations focus on making those high-profit items incrementally bigger, more powerful, and more efficient. Those incremental improvements enable the company to maintain the profit margin they are accustomed to achieving, yet provide enough improvement that existing customers will continue to purchase the product.

Unfortunately, incremental innovations are not disruptive innovations. That makes companies vulnerable to the disruptive innovations that emerge in the murky, low end of the market. Disruptive innovation is driven by the need to find cheaper methods to make a new product equal to the high-end products. Smart companies fail because they do everything right, according to what the schools of business say they should be doing, missing the disruptive innovations. Where do you think textbook publishers land on this continuum?

This is the philosophy that has driven Silicon Valley. Andy Grove, retired from Intel, credits this concept with the health and growth of Intel over the last fifteen years. Intel was leaving the low-end profit margin market for processors to AMD and Citrix, concentrating on their high-end desktop and server chips. He refocused the company, and the low-profit-margin Celeron processor chip blew AMD and Citrix out of the water—that processor is the highest volume product in the company.

Think of the iPad as related to a laptop computer. It does *most* of what a laptop can do, does it better, does it cheaper, not to mention it does it much more elegantly. Though changes are occurring that bring laptops or laptop-like netbooks down in price, all of those devices are being created in response to the iPad and its family of products.

Back to outlining how your district can transition from traditional textbooks to digital content *and* purchase computing devices for every student. The one condition is that your district must have line items in the operating budget for annual textbook and computer refresh purchases. If you do not have those, it will be very hard to determine the funds available for the transition.

For the purposes of illustration, we will use a school district with three thousand students as our model. We will also assume they have two hundred teachers and building administrators. Each teacher and administrator has a computing device and the district has been successful in reaching a student to computer ratio of 5:1, six hundred student computers. They are refreshing those eight hundred computers (student, teacher, and administrator devices) once every five years, meaning 156 devices replaced each year at an average cost of $600. Their annual textbook expenditure is $50/student. That means they are expending $93,600 for computing devices refresh and $150,000 for textbooks, a total of $243,600 per year.

Now we shift the process. All teacher and student devices are now wireless, web-browser-based units costing between $250 (netbook) and $300 (tablet); we will use $275 as the average cost per device. Chapter 9 will outline the rationale behind the assumptions behind student and teacher devices. We will need to subscribe to one of the low-cost web-browser classroom-management systems and inexpensive content, and that will cost you $15 per student per year.

We need to purchase 3,200 computing devices and we will phase the implementation over four budget cycles (four years). For the first two budget cycles, you take the computer refresh and textbook allocations and place most of the allocation in reserve for future purchases. In the second budget cycle you really should pilot the digital delivery system in ten classrooms, an estimated cost of $75,000. At the start of the third budget cycle, we subscribe to our digital resources for everyone, $45,000. We expend the remaining $610,000 and purchase approximately 2,200 student and teacher computing devices. We already had 220 devices for the pilot project and in the fourth cycle you purchase the remainder of the computing devices required. You now have a computing device for every student and teacher without increasing your budget. The realigned allocation then provides the computing device refresh required on an annual basis.

If you need to pay for an upgrade of your data network and install a high-density wireless network, that should not cost more than $360,000 for the total system. If your vendor wants more, you are working with the wrong vendor. You would then stretch the transition over six budget cycles. That works very well in that you will not need to start the computing device refresh cycle until your seventh budget cycle.

School districts with construction programs have an even easier time. The construction program represents a large, one-time allocation of funds. Buried in your construction budget are categories you would re-align for other purposes. Your hardwired data cable costs and associated switch data ports should be reallocated to the high-density wireless network costs. You have desktop student and teacher computers with a table and chair representing a budget of at least $800 on the low side, which are reallocated to purchasing wireless, web-browser student and teacher computing devices.

You can purchase three of those devices for the cost of one desktop computer with monitor, keyboard, mouse, table, and chair. When you add the existing textbook allocations and computer refresh funds to the reallocated construction funds, they represent the ability to provide a computing device for every student and shift to a digital instructional delivery system. It is a game changer.

Unfortunately, at least one state has placed all textbook purchases on hold for the next five years. That state is pursuing development of products by the large publishers and the state will provide the product to their school districts. The state received a large education grant and is using that as the fund source for the project.

That strategy does not appear to be financially sustainable. They have focused on the large existing publishers, who expect to continue with the profit level from the high end of the publishing market, textbooks—completely missing the innovations driven by the low-margin bottom of the market.

The real issue is that education will not be receiving any new sources of revenue or increases in current revenue streams any time soon. By eliminating the funds for textbooks, that state has just crippled the ability of its school districts to fund computing devices for every student. Another unfortunate fact is that some states have very restrictive rules and regulations regarding what can be purchased using textbook funds, prohibiting the scenario outlined above.

It would be too complex to attempt to provide guidelines for how much money needs to be allocated to specific categories. There are some ratios for technical support personnel suggested in the next chapter and you can develop some models using those suggestions. The purpose of this section is to bring awareness that student-centered twenty-first-century learning and teaching has a profound impact on your operating budget. A successful transition from a teacher-centered to student-centered twenty-first-century learning and teaching environment will require you to address funding issues. Leaving these issues unresolved and without specific strategies for funding the required changes, your Creating a Culture of Learning Plan with Roadmap is guaranteed to fail.

Assessment Questions Associated with the "Policies and Processes" Silo:

- Where in the organizational structure is the technical support department located?
- If not under curriculum and instruction, who does tech support answer to?
- If not under curriculum and instruction, are there any defined and articulated connection points and channels between curriculum and instruction and tech support?

- Does the district have a "Keeper of the Plan" for twenty-first-century learning and teaching?
- If so, where in the organizational structure is that person located?
- What is that person's level of authority in the structure?
- Does the district have a formal communication process horizontally across departments regarding curriculum and instruction or technology initiatives?
- Does the district have a formal communications process vertically from the district level, to the building level, to the classroom level and back up to district?
- Does the district have a formal software adoption process in place?
- Does the district have a formal hardware adoption process in place?
- Does the district have a TQM process for instructional quality in place?
- Does that process use the instructional management systems for its data points? If not, what does it use?
- Does the district track curriculum and instruction and technology expenditures in sufficient detail to ascertain historical trends?
- If so, obtain that data. (See chapter 10: The Planning Process.)

NOTES

1. Michael E. Gerber, *The E-Myth Revisited* (New York: HarperCollins, 2001).
2. National Center for Education Statistics, http://nces.ed.gov/.
3. Clayton Christensen, *The Innovator's Dilemma* (Cambridge, MA: The Presidents and Fellows of Harvard College, 1997; New York: HarperBusiness, 2000).

Chapter 6

Technical Support

As school districts transition to a student-centered twenty-first-century learning and teaching environment, technical support becomes even more important to a sustainable student-centered environment. An efficient and effective technical-support structure for student-centered twenty-first-century learning and teaching may look a bit different from your current technical-support structure. The following best practices are processes observed in other school districts modified by the author as an adaptation focused on student-centered twenty-first-century learning and teaching.

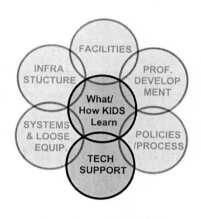

You will also find an overview of an international standard your district should be using with regard to how you integrate Information and Computer Technology (ICT) support into your organization. This chapter is all about creating a culture of support in your district. You will find that I use the term "systems support" to include your IT department. In today's integrated world, networking is central to almost all low-voltage systems used in the K–12 environment.

ORGANIZATIONAL STRUCTURE

A twenty-first-century technology support department has two distinct types of people in it; *People* people and *Things* people. I define a *People* person as someone who gains energy through the interface with other people. A *Things* person is someone who feels that it takes effort and energy to interface with other people. What types of gifts do you like the most for your birthday or Christmas?

A *Things* person will consistently land on the side of a new golf club, a fishing reel, music, or Amazon gift card for their e-reader. The point is that there are people in your technical support group who can talk to the file server and understand what the file server says when it talks back. They are *Things* people. However, sending that person to the classroom to assist a teacher who is starting to utilize student-centered twenty-first-century learning and teaching concepts will not work. Technical support includes some *People* people in the group who are available to assist teachers with adopting student-centered twenty-first-century learning and teaching concepts and processes.

Districts have started calling them learning and teaching coaches and they are the people who provide job-embedded professional development for teachers in their classrooms.

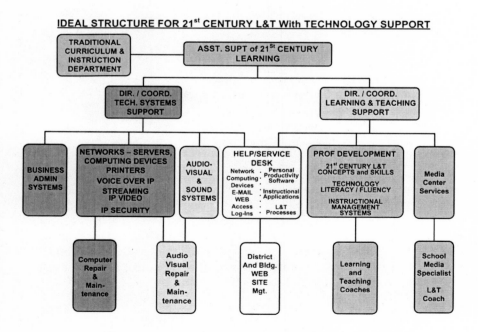

IDEAL STRUCTURE FOR 21st CENTURY L&T With TECHNOLOGY SUPPORT

The diagram has the technical support *People* people and *Things* people merged into one department that works under the curriculum and instruction division.

You may notice that the two sides meet at the service desk. A more detailed overview of what a service desk should look like and how it should function will follow an exploration of the functions and people who make up technical support.

LEARNING AND TEACHING SUPPORT

Learning and teaching support assists instructional staff in adopting student-centered twenty-first-century learning and teaching concepts, processes, and practices. This group has the responsibility for providing professional development and determining the training needs of instructional and administrative staff. They analyze the adequacy of available professional-development resources and coordinate and conduct professional-development activities.

This group who develops the specific Scope and Sequence Matrices of professional development for the district. They should also be taking the lead on the assessment and selection of classroom management tools required to enable teachers meet their mission of learning and teaching rubric.

They also model exemplary practices in student-centered twenty-first-century instructional delivery in the classroom with the teacher. Job-embedded user support is an extension of the staff professional-development plan and is meant to provide assistance for adopting student-centered twenty-first-century learning and teaching. For user support to be the most effective, it must occur at the building site, eventually involving all of the stakeholders at each site. The districts that have been successful in implementing a more student-centered learning environment with embedded technology have a ratio of one learning and teaching coach for every one hundred teachers.

Your response may be, "We cannot afford to increase our staff by that many people." You may already have them on staff. Most districts already have personnel in this category but they are typically called the instructional technology department or instructional specialists. Districts have reviewed their current staff and realized that there are a number of existing positions which should transition to learning and teaching coaches. Some examples:

- *Curriculum Specialists*—When you review the CCS, it is very clear that understanding the curriculum also means you understand student-centered twenty-first-century instructional delivery. This may require training, but your curriculum specialists should be able to articulate and demonstrate student-centered twenty-first-century learning and teaching.

- *Content Specialists*—One district had a small army of reading and math literacy coaches. When the district actually looked at what CCS expected regarding reading and math, it was apparent that these specialists really needed to be learning and teaching coaches, not simply literacy coaches. The CCS takes a much more integrated approach to learning and does not isolate content areas from each other.
- *Existing Technology Integration or Instructional Technology Specialists*— This goes back to the concept that this process is not about technology; it is about learning and teaching. All of these positions should be transitioned to learning and teaching coaches.
- *Media Specialists*—A more recent graduate with a media specialist certification is much more valuable as a learning and teaching coach than someone who manages your media center. Your district would benefit from hiring a noncertified person to actually "manage" your media center, which would free up your media specialist to use his or her training and be a learning and teaching coach for his or her building.

Those districts who have been successful in reorienting their faculty have found that a ratio of one learning and teaching coach for every one hundred teachers seems to be an effective, efficient, and sustainable guideline.

Directors of learning and teaching play a major role in ensuring that technology acquisitions are driven by the student experience requirements. They must have a strong background in twenty-first-century instructional delivery. They work hand in hand with the technology-systems support director to ensure that both sides of the technical support structure understand and execute their activities from the viewpoint that it is about learning and teaching, not technology. It is very important that there are no artificial barriers between the director of learning and teaching and director of technology systems and their staffs.

There are some individuals out there who can merge the learning and teaching AND technology-systems-support director positions into one person. They are rare and unique but when a district finds someone who understands technology at a deeper level but also has a deep understanding and experience of student-centered twenty-first-century learning and teaching, it is a great thing for the district.

TECHNOLOGY SYSTEMS SUPPORT

We need to make sure everyone is on the same page when the phrase "technology systems support" is used. If you review the diagram at the beginning of the chapter, you will see that it is not only IT (computing devices, servers, and networks). It also includes instructional technology, communication systems, and IP security. All of those systems use the network; therefore, most districts are moving them over to the IT department area of responsibility out of the traditional maintenance and operations area of responsibility.

During the transition there may be quite a few questions regarding who the teacher or principal calls to have a specific problem resolved with one of the systems on the campus. When we talk about the service desk later in the chapter, these systems must be covered by that software even if the actual repair work is done by an outside contractor working through a service agreement.

As outlined in the prior chapter, curriculum and instruction is the primary client of a systems support department. It is surprising how many times curriculum respond to inquiries about various operations with, "Systems support says we cannot do that." If systems support was a business and was not able to meet the needs of its primary customer, the primary customer would find an alternate source of support and the original company would be out of business.

There may be reasons for tensions in your district between a nontechnological director of curriculum and the director of systems support. However, as noted earlier, the primary reason systems support exists is curriculum. There will always be the need to create a culture of dialogue, articulation of expectations, and definition of costs and hindrances.

We also need to be honest with ourselves; one of the biggest hindrances to the quality of skill sets in your technology systems support department is pay scale. The K–12 environment is structured to pay more for those people who have more letters attached to their name and number of years of experience. The IT world pays based on what you can do, not how much you have been educated or how long you have been around. Those are two radically different approaches.

The higher-level networking skills required for high-density wireless networks, enabling BYOD and the associated security, and making the experience appear to be simple enables a network administrator to earn $125,000 to $200,000 in corporate America. That is equal to or more than many superintendents make and it simply will not happen in a K–12 organization. Even basic network administrators can make more money in corporate America than many teachers are paid in the K–12 environment.

Today's reality is that most districts will need "augmentation services" for someone with those skills and it will cost you $300 per hour or more for that person to work in your district. Some districts have unrealistic expectations of what their systems support people should be able to accomplish and will say, "We do not need that kind of expensive help."

On the other side of the coin, you have systems support personnel who believe they should be able to do anything that needs to be done and take personal offense when it is suggested the department needs assistance. Unfortunately, they end up learning on the job and the project they work on is a pain to everyone involved. The large majority of school districts need outside augmentation services to implement the high-density wireless required for student-centered twenty-first-century learning and teaching. It is simply part of the cost associated with doing business in the twenty-first century.

The second hindrance of importance regarding technology support within a K–12 organization is that most systems support departments are not managed from a structured process viewpoint. As the prior chapter mentioned about TQM and Michael Gerber's comment "You cannot manage people because people are irrational, but you can manage processes."

Most systems support groups are not following one of the internationally recognized management structures for IT. They are managed on a homegrown "squeakiest wheel/helter-skelter" reactive management process, responding to what happens to them rather than proactively managing their responsibilities.

If you do not manage from a structure process, there is no basis for discussions based on a rational process that identifies costs of and hindrances to a requested initiative. At best the department is guessing as to how to fill the request and you end up with its members learning as they go, creating user turmoil and frustration. At worst, they say they cannot do it because they are concerned about how it would affect their ability to juggle the balls they already have in the air.

The following is an overview of what one of those IT-structured management processes look like. For those with an education background, this will fall way outside your area of expertise. However, it is crucial for you to understand that there are structured management processes for IT and you need a cursory understanding of what they mean to your organization.

The leadership of most of the organizations in corporate America and corporate Europe was in the same boat as the leadership of K–12 organizations. Technology and IT was this thing out there that they really did not understand. They knew it used organization funds and had a number of people within the department.

However, they had no knowledge of how to manage the IT silo or even determine if what IT was doing aligned with the corporate goals and strategies of the organization. They only knew when things were not right; a lot of turmoil in the organization. Most executive-level people in the K–12 environment view technology in a similar manner.

What did corporate America and Europe do? It actually started with corporate Europe and more specifically with a department of the government of the United Kingdom. The UK Central Computer and Telecommunications Agency (CCTA), which merged into the Office of Government Commerce, started collecting processes representing the best practices for managing IT in 1989. That collection has grown into what is now called the Information Technology Services Management (ITSM) with the actual processes and description of how they work being called the Information Technology Infrastructure Library (ITIL).

It has spread from the UK, across Europe, and over to the United States. ITSM appears to be the most widely adopted best practices for IT and has the largest collection of corporate practitioners making it the international standard.

There are a number of competing IT management processes, such as: the Information Services Procurement Library (ISPL), the Application Services Library (ASL), Dynamic Systems Development Method (DSDM), and Control Objectives for Information and related Technology (COBIT). None of those have reached market penetration at the level of ITSM.

To assist you with understanding what ITSM represents, the following are some of the key concepts of how ITSM talks about its process. "The ITSM starts with and reinforces the key message that IT services are there solely to support the business and its efficient and effective operation. The three objectives of ITSM are: (1) To align IT services with the current and future needs of the business and its customers; (2) To improve the quality of the IT services delivered; (3) To reduce long-term cost of service provision. These goals would be the same for an educational organization."[1]

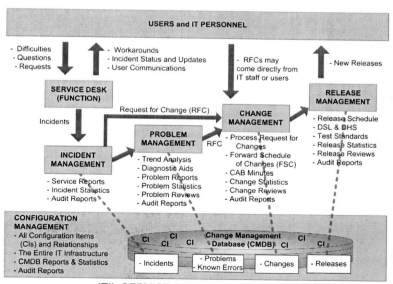

ITIL SERVICE SUPPORT PROCESSES

The ITIL philosophy adopts a process-driven approach that is scalable to fit both large and small IT organizations. It considers service management to consist of a number of closely related and highly integrated processes.

A key concept of ITIL management revolves around the definition of "customers" and "users." Customers are the persons paying for or authorizing an IT service; therefore they are the only group with the authority to enter into service agreements with the IT department. Users are the persons using an IT service.

These processes must use the people, tools, and technology effectively, efficiently, and economically in the delivery of high-quality, innovative IT services aligned to business processes. The overall structure divides the processes into two categories. As shown in the diagram, ITIL service support focuses on the day-to-day operational processes of the IT organization.

The ITIL service delivery processes are considered more tactical in focus, typically aligning to the longer term IT service goals and objectives of an organization.

You do not need to fully understand all of the pieces of ITSM; you need to know that there is a highly regarded, logical, sequential set of processes

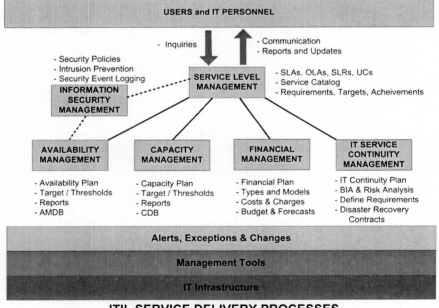

ITIL SERVICE DELIVERY PROCESSES

out there. It is used by corporate America to pull IT out of its isolated silo and align it with the goals and strategies of the organization. Executives of corporate America do not need to know what IT actually does; they only need to know how to interpret the data that comes out of the ITSM process.

A rational, process-based management structure is a necessity. Of all of the processes, ITSM has the largest number of organizations that have adopted its process, and it is the one you should use. Your entire IT department should be certified in the ITSM process. It takes at least two years to reorient an IT department to the ITSM standards once the training has begun.

Before we move away from technology systems support, we need to address the quantity and type of personnel who should be in the department. Most experts agree that educational organizations have less stringent support requirements than corporate America. A qualified technical person will typically support 750 computing devices in an educational environment, while corporate America expects a ratio of 150 computing devices per technical support person.

At this point in time, we do not have enough information to quantify any statement regarding how many of these web-browser-based devices are to be managed by one technical support person. We do know that they require much less attention, implying that one person can manage many more of those devices than desktop PCs, but there are no firm ratios available. Perhaps three thousand devices per each technical support person is a reasonable ratio to start with.

Then you have your network administrators, specialists who set up and configure the hard-wired and wireless networks for the users. There are server specialists who keep the servers and their applications up and running. Then there are specialists for Voice over Internet Protocol (VoIP) phone systems. There are no industry standards regarding ratios of those specialists within educational organizations.

The quantity required within each school district has a wide range of variance dependent upon sophistication of the networks and how modern of an application it is running on a server. Older applications are much more labor intensive to maintain than more modern versions. The highest-skill-level people in this category are the ones suggested you need to bring in from an external resource.

In today's K–12 environment, we cannot exclude the audio, AV, and security system technicians from the technology systems support discussion. More and more of those systems are utilizing the data network as part of how the system works or access the control of the system via the data network. In the smaller school districts, it may be more effective to pay a "priority service rate" to a qualified contractor rather than training a staff member. Larger districts should bring that type of expertise into the fold.

Most school district personnel are not aware that industry trade associations provide certifications for all of the industries associated with the systems serviced by the technology systems support group. Hiring a person with a certificate does not guarantee they can actually execute and deliver the required services but the district has a much higher chance that a certified person has the knowledge and skills required.

For basic computer setup, and operation, look at the CompTIA.org certifications. Networking, router, wide area network, and higher-level server functions certification are also located at CompTIA.org and the International Electrical and Electronic Engineers, IEEE.org. Audio and AV system certification for the required skills and knowledge are available from InfoComm.org. Security system certifications for technicians are available from the Electronic Security Association, esaweb.org. You may have noticed that vendor-specific certifications are not listed. The generic knowledge and skills are prerequisites of vendor-specific training.

SERVICE DESK

At the beginning of this chapter we brought back the ideal technical-support organizational structure diagram from chapter 5; please take a look at it again. Please note that technology systems support and learning and teaching support meet at the service desk. Unfortunately, most districts use what they call the "help desk," limited to IT functions only. A fully functional service desk is a bidirectional communications channel for everything related to learning and teaching and all technology, not just IT. It should also be an ITIL-compliant software application.

Before assisting you with understanding what a good service desk looks like, we need to define what it should not look like. There will be questions in the assessments related to the service desk at the end of the chapter but these concepts will help you understand those questions.

It is safe to make the assumption that your technology systems support and learning and teaching support are not working a service desk jointly. They are separate groups of people and only the IT people actually use some type of "help desk" software. It would also be safe to assume that your intercom, paging systems, sound systems, clocks, and bells are not handled through IT; they are external contractors most likely being called in by your maintenance and operations people.

Security systems fall in the same category. Perhaps your phone system is now under IT, but that is a recent change and the addition of servicing projectors and classroom AV systems is also very recent. Knowing who to call can be a bit of an issue. If you have not realized it, things should not be separated this way. All of those functions should be under the umbrella of a single service desk

Most of the school districts have an "IT help desk" based around the concept of service tickets. There is a major efficiency component reflected by whether you have a policy requiring users to create service requests electronically. If users can simply stop a service person in the hallway, you are bypassing the power and efficiency a true service desk can bring to your operation. This is a different way of doing business but it is a necessity. We need to have a knowledge base of what is happening with technology in the district and that requires only electronic requests so everything can be logged and analyzed.

A second efficiency issue is "Who creates a service request?" Can users create a service request or can only the help desk create service requests? The proper method is that the user creates a service request via logging into the service desk via their web browser and filling out a service request form electronically. The technician reviews the issue and determines if it is an "incident" or something that can be solved without involving the user in the process; for instance, sending an e-mail pointing the user to a support document or video that instructs the user how to do what he or she needs to do. We want all service requests logged but not all service requests are elevated to become an "incident"-level event.

Another observation is that the response to service tickets is more of an ad hoc process where the "squeakiest" problem is handled first. Ask your help desk people about the process they use to prioritize service tickets. Then ask for a print out of service requests for the last thirty days. Take a look at the duration for a response time and solution and see if that prioritization process has been followed.

No? Then service is being delivered on a "squeakiest wheel first" basis. A side note, you should have the prioritization process and definition of levels reviewed and approved by the executive cabinet.

The last major issue to discuss is whether service requests are managed from a structured or nonstructured viewpoint. Ask the question: "How do you determine there are groups of incidents that represent a larger problem?" They should answer with: "We run an application once a week that looks at all 'incidents' and groups them by user, groups of users, or computing devices with similar configurations. We then target the user or groups of users with targeted training. If we have a number of computing devices with similar configuration experiencing similar problems, they are grouped together and elevated to what we call 'problem management'." Any answer other than something similar means your IT Department I managed from an unstructured basis, typically more of helter-skelter model servicing the squeakiest wheel first.

Now we will turn to the definition of a properly functioning service desk. At the base, foundational level of an ITIL-compliant service desk is the change management database. The database contains what ITIL calls "configuration items." Configuration items are details about all of the components that make up the technology environment of the organization. That entails both the physical components and application components. In some ways, it is an asset-management system but with quite a bit more detail (granular), and it also has what are called "mother–daughter relationships."

An example: a computing device is broken down into components like the model and version of motherboard, what type and version of BIOS (Basic Input Output System, which the firmware uses when the device wakes up) is on the motherboard, what type and model of CPU, how much and what type of RAM memory, what type and size of hard drive, what operating system (what version of Windows, etc.), and what applications are on the device.

Within the database we create what are called mother–daughter relationships. The motherboard has a relationship to the BIOS, to the processor, to memory, to hard-drive capacity, to operating system, and so on.

The power of creating this database and the mother–daughter relationships comes into to play when the day-to-day ITIL-based incident management (trouble ticket) runs a report and finds that ten computing devices with the same configuration items are experiencing network log-in problems. The technical support people elevate the issue to a problem management issue and work to find a solution.

When the solution is found or a workaround developed, they go back to the change management database and run a report to identify all other computing devices with the same configuration items. The department can then schedule to touch all of those other devices and install the fix before the users experience the failure the first ten users experienced. How's that for a proactive IT management scenario?

Let's expand the concept beyond IT over to instructional technology. The change management database has the projector, video presentation tool, classroom integrated AV system, and so on as configuration items. Users report all problems with these systems to the service desk. A report generated by the incident management systems indicates that a number of users have experienced a problem with switching between the presentation computer and a document camera when using the classroom integrated AV system from manufacturer X.

That issue is elevated to problem management where technology systems support finds a solution and proactively implements the solution for all other classroom-integrated AV systems from that manufacturer. Think of how this would apply to projector problems.

Let's expand this one more level to cover the actual applications available to all users. Service desk requests for help have both technology systems support and learning and teaching coaches responding to requests for help. Access to learning and teaching coaches is like being referred to a specialist of any service center you call. The request is first responded to by a service desk technician, who verifies the issue and classifies it as an application issue.

That technician can take a look to see if a learning and teaching coach is available (logged onto the system). If one is not available, the system will place that incident report (trouble ticket) into a queue for the next learning and teaching coach who logs on.

The real power for expanding your service desk, merging systems support and learning and teaching support, is that you can run reports on your incidents and look for trends. It does not matter if the incident trend applies to a computing device, network hardware, AV hardware, or an application. If the report indicates a number of users are having issues with a specific application or aspect of an application, the learning and teaching support team should see there are multiple incidents of a similar nature.

They can then plan a professional-development event or function, or develop an online tutorial that targets training to assist users with that application. Or professional development is targeted and delivered to a specific group of users. Oh my! We are being effective and efficient solving user problems when they occur regardless of whether the problem is associated with a computing device, the network, the applications being used, or the AV equipment located in classrooms. This is what a service desk should be doing.

DISASTER RECOVERY AND SERVICE CONTINUITY PLAN

Buried within the ITIL process is a process called IT service continuity management. While it is part of the ITIL standard and the importance of those processes have been documented, this one item is important enough to pull out as a separate item. When you ask members of your technology systems support department if they have a disaster recovery plan, there is little doubt they will respond, "Yes." This is an IT policy, and unfortunately we need to dig a bit deeper because most plans are found to be inadequate when an actual disaster occurs. We will address the data and applications side of the issue, leaving the AC power redundancy to chapter 8.

There are a number of things systems support must do before even creating a Disaster Recovery and Service Continuity Plan (DRSCP). The first step is to conduct an inventory of all applications and verify with each department any database the department needs to be backed up and made available after a disaster. All applications should have a set of media (DVD or even mobile hard drive) from the manufacturer stored in a magnetic and fireproof safe/vault, not on a shelf in the technology systems support office. In addition to the applications, a complete record of all user IDs and passwords used with any application should also be in that same storage location.

A complete list of the data that needs to be backed up is compiled and determination made of how that will occur. Part of the plan should also define where that backup data will be located. It should not be in the same facility where the database and related application is located. It must be somewhere different.

The plan should also have a written component that defines the actual sequence of events as the systems are brought back online. It will take a bit of thinking and planning to get the sequence correct. Bringing an application and its related database back online without having security for who can access the information can be embarrassing.

Now that you have a plan, test it! Yes, intentionally cause things to fail and execute the plan. Does the plan actually work? The only way to know is to test it under real conditions. A cautious way to test the DRSCP is to test in pieces; that is, bring down a portion of the system as if it failed and see if the DRSCP enables you to restore that service. A caution is that you are not truly testing your sequence of the restart of everything.

Your DRSCP should be updated each quarter and tested on an annual basis.

AUTOMATED PROCESSES

As we review where the industry is heading regarding wireless networks, it becomes apparent there are various applications which automate a number of IT functions. They have a tremendous impact on the efficiency of your technology-systems support group and the users.

Too many technical support groups function as the gatekeeper for resetting and reissuing user ID and passwords. Really? How many people would you need to expand that group when every student has a computing device? There is no reason why anyone in technical support should be involved with that function other than setting up the parameters of how your automated user ID and password system works. I will caution you that how user IDs and passwords for preschool or PreK through second grade are automated should be different from the third-graders and up; the teacher will need to be somewhere in the loop for those younger students.

The second automated process you should have is a single-user ID and password application. For the most part this application is for your staff, though there may be situations where high-school students would need multiple user IDs and passwords. The concept is that the main user ID and password of a user is all that person needs to use for access to all of the places he or she goes.

Implementing one of these applications can be harder, because it is not simply installing the application for internal use, but how old are the applications the users need to access and will they allow the automation? There are some web-based applications that are so old that they also do not allow automation. Each district will encounter different problems with automating single-user ID and password dependent upon the applications you use and resources your staff needs to access.

The last one is a tougher one and will require expenditures for software, perhaps hardware, and one of those external specialists you pay $300/hour to set up the system. The concept is called network log-in and authentication; which contains mobile-device management. There are a number of different approaches to how you can accomplish the task. Your users already log in to your network, but this is something much more intense and powerful.

This function is something every school district in the country needs to implement for proper security and resource allocation, especially when wireless networks are the primary method for connecting computing devices.

Think of the problem from this viewpoint: your young children go outside to play during the summer. They run around, sweat, and who knows what they have picked up and handled. At our house, we would have them wash their hands before they even eat a snack and a number of times, feed them dinner outside. Then we would require them to go straight to the bathroom and take a bath (with soap) before we would allow them to touch or sit on much of anything in the house.

You have the same issue with mobile devices, regardless of whether they are district owned or a BYOD device the student or teacher brings from home. You must first determine if they are clean before you allow them on the network. Then you must be able to control and block undesirable applications or files on those devices from running or connecting to your network.

The concept is that the network has intelligence that takes into account your user ID and password *plus* the device you are using to log in on. It controls what comes from the device onto the network and provides a very detailed (granular) control of where that user can go on the network and what resources are available to that specific user based on the device he or she is using.

If a person visits your campus and the network system does not know who that person is and does not recognize the computing device, the only thing that person can access is a tunnel through your system to the Internet. The person will not be able to see anything on your system or connect to any of your resources. Nothing from his or her device will be allowed to download or connect to anything on your network—everything is blocked.

Let's change it up: you are a student who brings a tablet from home. The system recognizes your user ID and password but does not recognize your tablet. The network will only allow you to connect to the Internet and access your personal resources located on the system (your files on the storage system). However, it will not allow you to run school applications and it will block anything it does not recognize coming from your device.

As a student who wants to bring their tablet to school, you want more access. First you install the correct threat-management suite (as required by the district) and register/authenticate your device with the school. Now, when you log on, you have access to all of the typical things students can have access to plus your personal files. The network still monitors what happens and blocks activities it does not recognize, but the student has access to everything they need and the network is protected.

Now you use one of the district mobile computing devices you took home last night to log in to the network. You have access to the regular student places, your personal files, plus access to special applications, but the network still monitors and blocks activities it does not recognize as valid functions, making sure you did not bring something in from outside the district.

The final variation is that the student is now using a school district desktop computing device that has AutoCAD, Photoshop, or some other application that cannot run in a web-browser environment. The network confirms that the student is authorized to log onto that device and monitors any external storage (think USB thumb drive) the student may connect to the desktop. If a teacher logs onto that same desktop, the teacher is allowed access to a completely different set of resources and applications, and the network still monitors files the teacher downloads directly on the desktop.

There is one user ID and password for all of the scenarios described but dependent on who you are and the computing device you are using, the network will flex and enable access to different resources and run different applications. It is not a simple yes or no as to whether you can or cannot log onto the network; it provides much more control of where and what the user can or cannot access and do.

We cannot finish this section without warning the reader that the web browser, public and private cloud computing environment has a large impact on network log-in and authentication. The best practices of how this will all work out can be observed at your local university or college. For whatever reason, corporate America is reinventing the wheel for what universities have already done. You may be better off talking with your local university IT department than your local vendor.

Assessment Questions Associated with the "Technical Support" Silo:

- Has the district developed the concept of learning and teaching coaches providing job-embedded professional development in the instructional space?
- If so, what is the ratio of learning and teaching coaches to instructional staff?
- If so, have they defined required competencies as defined by a Professional-Development Scope and Sequence Matrix?
- If not, are there existing positions (technology integration, curriculum specialists, content literacy specialists, media specialists, or other) that the district could transition into learning and teaching coaches?
- Does the technology systems support have responsibility for paging, sound systems, classroom-integrated AV, clocks, and security video cameras?
- Does the district engage external IT consultants for implementing higher-level functions in the district?
- What quantity of personnel performs what tasks for the technical systems support group?
- Has the district implemented a structured management process for the support group? If so, which process are they using?
- Has any of the support staff been certified for that process? If so, what percentage of the group membership?
- If the district has implemented a structured management process, assess how the department adheres to those standards for every primary and secondary process identified in the process.
- Has the district defined required skill sets and knowledge for personnel based on the various trade association certifications? If so, what are those certifications?
- Does the district have a traditional IT help desk or "merged" service desk providing incident support for IT, all technology, and applications?
- If traditional IT help desk, are all users required to log requests electronically?
- If traditional IT help desk, are service requests elevated to incidents? If so, who elevates the issues to an actual incident-level event?
- If traditional IT help desk, what is the prioritization process used to classify urgency of requests?

- If traditional IT help desk, are incidents grouped and elevated to problem management? If so, how does this occur?
- If service desk, how does the district enable access to learning and teaching coaches?
- Has technology systems support migrated to virtualized servers?
- Has technology systems support migrated to network storage? If so, describe the systemic approach.
- Has technical systems support automated setup of user ID and password?
- Has technical systems support automated single-user ID?
- Has technical systems support implemented network log-in and authentication?
- Does it include mobile-device management?

NOTE

1. *IT Service Management*, Version 2.1.b MacFarlane, Ivor and Rudd, Cavin. Cambray, Derek (Editor), 2005. itSMF Ltd., Reading, United Kingdom

Chapter 7

Student-Centered Learning Spaces

Typical of previous chapters, the best practices herein are a compilation of various sources. Those sources include best practices for educational-facility design as documented in various white papers, presentations, and guidelines from the Council of Educational Facility Planners International (CEFPI.org). The American National Standards Institute (ANSI) and internationally recognized Telecommunications Industry Association/Electronics Industry Association (TIA/EIA) standards for spaces where data network 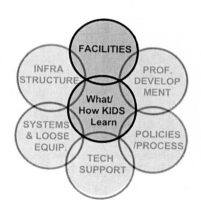 hardware is located and all cabling is collected together and terminated. It also includes best practices as observed by the author from various school districts, educational planners, and architects.

FACILITIES AND STUDENT-CENTERED TWENTY-FIRST-CENTURY LEARNING AND TEACHING

Before we get into the best practices observed regarding facilities and student-centered twenty-first-century learning and teaching, we need to walk through a review of a typical school-building life cycle and its implications for most school districts. The first statement is that student-centered twenty-first-century learning and teaching can take place virtually anywhere. The concepts and processes are not limited to a specific type of space or size of space.

Yes, the efficiency of the processes can be impacted by the amount of space and type of furniture you have in your classrooms, but that type of learning can still occur. This is a very good thing because most school districts will be implementing student-centered twenty-first-century learning and teaching in existing classrooms rather than new classrooms.

School buildings have traditionally used commercial-grade materials in their construction process, resulting in buildings with a usable life of seventy to eighty years, barring acts of God and fire. Many school districts will execute some type of renovation on a building between thirty and forty years after the facility is first placed in use. Typically, that renovation will replace the HVAC system for improved air quality, energy efficiency, and noise reduction, which means the ceilings and lights have to come down and be replaced.

It may also include recovering walls but it does not include moving of walls. The building will have the same basic layout for most of the time the school district uses it as a learning facility. Why is it important to understand that a typical school building lasts seventy to eighty years?

It means that even in the best of economic times, it takes ten years for school districts in the United States to replace only 12.5 percent of the total number of classrooms. In the same ten-year time frame, we are renovating and updating another 12.5 percent of our older facilities. The economy of the last five years has dropped those percentages down to less than 5 percent.

Another factor to take into account is that the majority of school facilities built in the last ten to fifteen years follow the "industrial learning" model, which leads to facilities designed with hallways and large standardized instructional spaces on each side of that hallway (double-loaded corridor design).

A teaching concept developed in the 1890s evolved into the Carnegie Unit approach to education, which later evolved into the "industrial learning" model. The Carnegie Unit approach expects a student will participate in approximately 180 instructional periods of fifty to sixty minutes each regarding a particular content area and the student will learn what they need to learn.

In the early 1900s, school designs enabled a more efficient delivery method of the concept, where content specialists (teachers) were provided with a space where they could store their instructional support collection for their content area and the students would move from room to room. That is what we define as the "industrial learning" model. The implied expectation is that every student learns at the same pace and in the same manner; we know that is not the case.

For the next forty years, these are the majority of spaces where students will experience student-centered twenty-first-century learning and teaching and teachers will learn how to facilitate those student experiences.

INSTRUCTIONAL SPACES AND STUDENT-CENTERED TWENTY-FIRST-CENTURY LEARNING AND TEACHING

There are books, research, white papers, and presentations generated by architects and educational facility planners that provide a much more in-depth analysis and more information than the conceptual overview contained in this section. Further research of information generated by those professionals may be of additional value to you.

School districts fortunate enough to have revenue sources for construction of new facilities have an opportunity to create instructional spaces that explicitly support and expect student-centered twenty-first-century learning and teaching experiences. When we review the concepts in chapter 1, student-centered twenty-first-century learning and teaching spaces should enable creation of small groups for students for discussions and collaboration on projects. Even collaboration between students from different classrooms would be advantageous. At the same time, we will still need a large presentation surface for students or the teacher to share information with a large group of learners in each large space.

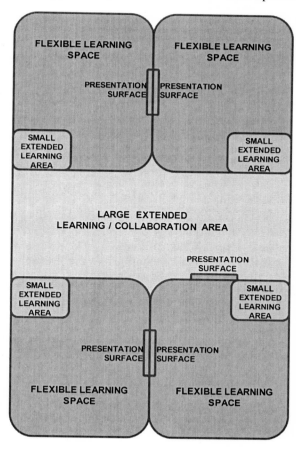

There are distinct differences in how this works out based on grade levels, which we will explore a little further on; however, the diagram provides a conceptual overview of the types of spaces which enhance a twenty-first-century learning experience.

Obviously, we have a larger learning space that flexes in its configuration throughout the day based on what student experiences are occurring in that space. We do need to point out the flexibility within the space is dependent on the type of furniture used in the space, which we deal with in the next section. The larger flexible learning space will be associated with smaller learning spaces (explicitly designed for small groups) and a large collaborative learning space. That large collaborative space is an extension of the flexible learning space.

The individual flexible learning spaces are intentionally smaller than current spaces, using that square footage to expand the hallway into the collaboration area. The number of flexible learning spaces to large collaborative space can be anywhere from four and up to eight, enabling various pod configurations. Now we have a very highly efficient set of spaces designed to flex with a large variety of student experiences. This arrangement does not require any more square footage than a set of four modern classrooms and hallway.

One of the primary features of these types of spaces is a requirement for clear sight lines (a lot of glass) from the flexible learning space to the small extended learning area and to the large extended learning/collaboration area. We have more spaces but we still have four teachers, and perhaps teaching assistants, to monitor student behavior in those spaces. Providing more clean sight lines enables the typical teacher to monitor more spaces.

Another feature, when coupled with a 2.5:1 student-to-student-computing-device ratio, is to provide smaller student device carts and place them in the collaborative area. When needed, a teacher can use those carts in his or her room and every student has a device. That will eliminate the need for a computer lab that students have to move to multiple times a week.

Districts that renovated older, 1960s through 1980s facilities with double-loaded corridors into a similar configuration have solved the space issue differently. Instead of making the hallway larger, they convert one out of four regular classrooms along the same hallway into a collaborative space and install glass between the remaining three classrooms and the collaborative space. To accommodate the same student population, they will typically add a wing to the building. That is more expensive than a replacement of the HVAC system and ceilings, but much less expensive than building a new facility.

We need to come back to the comment that there are differences to these configurations based on grade levels. The reality is that PreK through second-grade students are learning how to function within a structured environment and the physical environment needs to reflect that reality.

Too many unstructured physical spaces simply confuse most students in those grade levels. On the other hand, as students become older, there is less need for structured spaces; they know how they should behave.

Middle-school students need less structure and high-school students need even less. If you take a hard look at PBL or STEM school facilities designed in the last five years, you will see more of a knowledge-based office environment than a double-loaded corridor school design. The point is that we should not assume that the type of physical environment that works for high-school students is the same physical environment that works best for second-graders or vice versa; their needs are radically different.

One of the earliest papers relating to the creation of flexible environments for high schools comes from Copa and Pease in 1992.[1] They build the case that to prepare students to compete globally, whether they attend college or move directly into a career, high schools must move away from the Carnegie Unit–based departmental high school. They develop the argument of how learning and teaching must change.

Then they specifically point to a design from educational facility planner Bruce Jilk, AIA, and designer Jim Shields, AIA, which broke a high school down into multiple 100-student "families" as an example of a space explicitly designed to support student-centered twenty-first-century learning and teaching. Each family area would contain twenty-five-student work spaces, a wet classroom (science), a dry classroom, and four teachers.

To accommodate larger student populations, you simply add more family blocks. A very interesting aspect of this design concept is that the amount of

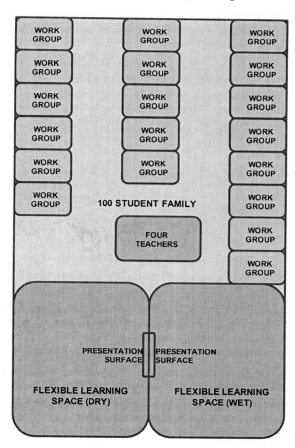

square footage required to implement this type of space is the same required for four typical high-school classrooms.

The design of the facility creates a very explicit physical environment
that requires teachers and students to change how learning occurs. That
learning methodology aligns very clearly with the new CCS and the 4 Cs.
Over the last decade, a number of high schools have been constructed that
follow this model. When coupled with changes in instructional delivery,
professional development, and policies and processes, student academic
achievement gains representing substantial increases are the typical outcome. Facilities can have a very distinct impact on the culture of learning
reflecting student-centered twenty-first-century learning and teaching in
your district.

In student-centered twenty-first-century learning and teaching, the
media center becomes more of a collaborative instructional space for
projects rather than research activities and reference materials. If you
have multiple student devices in the classroom, those devices have access
to the same research and reference sites as the student devices located in
the media center.

Typically, there are applications that require more computing power
than what a student or teacher device can deliver; that is, video or photo
editing (I would not be surprised to see those move to cloud/web-
browser based applications in the future), and those are located in or near
the media center.

As noted in chapter 6, media specialists coming out of colleges and
universities today are content and technology specialists. They are better
utilized as learning and teaching coaches than the organizer of the media
center shelves. The media center of today needs to have flexible learning
space(s), collaboration areas, and small-group areas. The quantity of each
type of those spaces is dependent on the grade levels housed in the facility and how many students the center serves, as well as the square footage
of the media center.

There are good reasons to have a discussion about how many books
should or should not be placed in the media center. Additional research
and discussion with qualified personnel would be of value. However, it is
important to note that the number of books sold in the United States has
shifted dramatically to e-reader books.

FURNISHINGS AND FURNITURE FOR STUDENT-CENTERED
TWENTY-FIRST-CENTURY LEARNING AND TEACHING

One look into a classroom can provide a tremendous amount of information regarding the student experience that occurs in that space. If the

student furniture is tablet armchairs aligned in orderly and neat rows, you can be assured that the teacher is the information gatekeeper using lectures to deliver content. If the inputs and controls for a large-screen projection system are located on the teacher's desk, it tells you that the system is a teacher tool that students do not access. The configuration and location of resources and furniture in the room will indicate if the space is a teacher-centered or student-centered environment.

Unfortunately, most new facilities are clearly teacher-centered environments. Even in the schematic design discussions, the owner and architect start with the "teaching wall." They do not understand that the concept of a teaching wall explicitly says there one person delivering information to many. It is a presentation concept. We are not stating that an instructional space does not need the capacity for one or two people to share information with all of the others in the space, but that is not the primary method for delivery of content.

Why does it need to be something as large as a wall? The answer reflects back to furniture. If the students are sitting in neat and orderly rows, the student farthest from the viewing/writing surface determines how large the writing or image must be. When it comes to projection of computer screens, the height of the image must be one-sixth of the distance to the farthest person viewing the image. If that farthest student is twenty feet from the image, the image must be forty inches tall. Measure the height of a chalk or marker board the next time you visit a classroom; you will find the height is around forty inches.

A STEM middle-school project was mentioned in the preface. During planning, the question was asked: "What is the value of a large-screen, wall-mounted projection system when the instructional process is project-based learning with students working primarily in a small, four- and five-student groups?" The answer came up: not as much value as we would like.

We then explored how to change the value proposition. The end result was that we used flexible furniture and technology for the solution; we reduce the distance from the farthest person viewing the image to the actual image. We would implement a large, fifty-five-inch, LCD flat-panel display with interactive touch capacity and a wireless computer workstation on a mobile cart that could be moved around the classroom for use by a specific group of students.

When those students or the teachers need to present information to everyone, the teacher simply says, "Move your chairs and gather around the display." Now our large presentation system has value for small-group projects and presentations to all people in the space. We are using spatial relationships, furniture, and technology to explicitly define the type of student experience we expect teachers to facilitate in their space.

Yes, you could move a small group of students to the wall-mounted presentation system, but we now need to address the question of where are the inputs and controls for the system. Before we answer that question, it is of value to understand that teachers from different grade levels have different attitudes regarding their "stuff."

The early-grade-level teachers seem to view all things in the classroom as resources to be used for student experiences, including the things on their desk, such as a computer. As you move up in grade level, there is less of that attitude. When you get to high-school teachers, the stuff on their desk cannot be touched by students. That begs the question, where do you install the AV system inputs and controls? If they are on the teacher's desk, the older students who would gain the most value from having access to a presentation system cannot access the system.

The key to student use of a wall-mounted presentation system is a piece of furniture where you can locate the inputs, controls, and ancillary devices separate from the teacher's desk. Even when that "Presentation Station" setup is not being used for a presentation, a small group of students can be using the computer and larger display (larger than a Chromebook or tablet) as a collaboration tool where multiple students can see and comment on the document or application they are using for their project.

Flexibility in your furniture is key. We need student chairs separate from student desks enabling reconfiguration of groups and functions within the room. Keep in mind that it appears the PreK to second-grade students perform better when there is a more explicit physical structure. That concept applies to furniture; PreK to second-grade rooms do not need furniture that can be easily reconfigured by the students.

Before we leave this section on furniture, it would be advantageous to point out that there is a substantial amount of empirical information regarding furniture and the human body. Specifically related to education, a European school furniture manufacturer has funded and conducted quite a bit of research. The findings are quite interesting.

One finding is that the body is constantly in motion, whether we realize it or not. Prove it to yourself. Stand up and close your eyes while paying attention to your body position. You will sense that your body is slightly swaying the entire time you stand. What we think of as standing still is actually filled with minute activity where your muscles are making slight adjustments the entire time you are standing. The really interesting thing is that those adjustments happen even while you are sitting down.

We do not need to purchase an expensive Steelcase Aeron task chair for students. However, you should not be purchasing any type of rigid chair design. Those chairs cause discomfort, which in turn cause students to fidget and eventually act out to relieve the discomfort. The chair must have some lateral and vertical flexibility; they are available at a price point the K–12 market can afford.

The same company also points out that correct chair and desk height is solely dependent on the height of the individual. The concept of one size fits all is most definitely not correct. The range in sizes among second-graders is much less than the range in size between sixth-graders but there are still differences. What that really means is that you should purchase a variety of sizes of desk/chair combinations for your building. At the beginning of each year, the teachers would negotiate with each other and trade out chair/desk combos to better match what their students need. Will it be perfect for every student? No. But you will be much closer to providing most students with appropriately sized desk/chair combos than a one-size-fits-all approach.

There is one more issue to visit with regard to furniture. The two assessment consortiums creating the annual summative assessments aligned with the CCS, PARCC and SABC, were mentioned in chapter 1. Both of the consortiums are requiring real-time online assessments displacing any type of paper-based assessments. There will be some political maneuvering for waivers in those states that have not yet conducted on-line assessments but eventually everyone will be using real-time, online assessments. Those states that have conducted real-time online assess-ments have found that they need to create classrooms in their facilities that can be reconfigured into assessment spaces for three or four weeks out of the school year.

The furniture selected for those spaces is also different. Typically, they are purchasing movable two-person desks with separate chairs. The desks have cable trays so AC power can be distributed to all computing device locations. (More about how we do that in chapter 8: The Hidden Support Systems.)

For those three or four weeks, the space is reconfigured as a testing lab and students are rotated in and out of the classroom as required to com-plete the total assessment for the student population of that facility. The quantity of these spaces is based solely on the student population, how many of those students must be assessed, and the time frame in which the assessments must be completed.

All of this implies that you need to add a budget for furniture replace-ment when you plan to renovate an older building. Yes, it is very hard to carve that extra money for furniture out of a limited budget. However, you are replacing your HVAC system primarily to increase efficiency. Replace your furniture and you will equally improve your efficiency for learning and teaching. Remember you will only need to replace the furni-ture in your third- through twelfth-grade rooms.

SPATIAL RELATIONSHIPS

This category could cover quite a bit of area but we will restrict ourselves only to those issues that have an impact on learning and teaching. We have already reviewed the concepts of spatial relationship between flexible learning spaces, small extended learning spaces, and collaboration spaces. We also took a look at what type of spatial relationships occur for the 100 Student Family concepts. We should discuss media centers and part of the unique functions they fulfill regarding student-centered twenty-first-century learning and teaching.

If you are moving toward a high ratio of student to student computing devices or even one-to-one, there will be applications such as photo and video editing that will not run on web-browser-based computing devices. As noted, those applications are typically operating on desktop computers located in the media center. That implies that the students would have to move from their instructional area to the media center to accomplish projects that required those applications.

Perhaps an alternate concept is to extend the media center out to the collaboration spaces. Placing a few desktop computing devices with the higher function applications in the collaborative learning space or a few of the cubicles of the 100 Student Family essentially extends the function of the media center out to the student locations.

Traditional industrial arts has been replaced with computer-based modeling, simulation, and curriculums that rotate students through exposure to a variety of industries at the middle-school level. High-school industrial arts are being replaced with higher-order modeling and simulation, computing device setup/repair and networking labs, and STEM labs. Even where machines are used, they are highly efficient computer numerically controlled (CNC) devices, requiring fewer devices and much less square footage housing those "dirty and noisy" processes.

If these technology curriculums are activities that most of the students will participate in, those spaces need to be centralized and easily accessible from the academic areas. They should not be located at the periphery of facilities similar to physical education and fine arts spaces.

Spatial relationships also come into play regarding "after-hours access." Are those special function technology labs and media center located in the facility where they can be accessed by students, and parents, after hours? Are they accessible without enabling students and parents to wander through other parts of the facility where you do not have school district personnel monitoring activities?

TECHNICAL SPACES

The last category of spaces to touch on is the spaces where your technology lives. We apologize that we have to move deep into the geek world of network cabling, but it is very important to utilize the national standards for data cabling and network technology. With specific regard to technology standards, you should be utilizing what are called the ANSI/TIA/EIA standards as follows:

- ANSI/TIA/EIA 568-C Series, Commercial Building Telecommunications Cabling Standard
- ANSI/TIA/EIA 569-A Series, Commercial Building Standards for Telecommunications Pathways and Spaces.
- ANSI/TIA/EIA 607—Grounding and Bonding

It is important to note that these standards address the specific needs of commercial buildings; educational facilities may have a few minor differences. The 568-C series provides the standards for all types of cabling, but it is the 569-A series that defines the space requirements for technology. The standards address two types of spaces. The first is what most people call the head-end room where the main components for most of all of the systems used in an educational facility are located.

They used to be called MDF (main distribution frames) but the standards have changed the term to TR (telecommunication room). The second type of space is called a TC (telecommunications closet), which used to be called an IDF, typically housing only cable terminations and data switch hardware.

There are some simple rules of thumb regarding all of these spaces:

- You should be able to enter the room from a public space (the technician should not have to enter a classroom to get to a TR or TC).
- The room is sized for the number of cabinets expected to be located in the room, and there is a minimum of thirty inches in front and to the rear of each cabinet with a minimum twenty-four inches to one side.
- The ceiling space is not used as a pathway for HVAC ducts or plumbing.
- A TR or TC is located within a 290-foot pathway from any cable port to the room or closet.
- The TR or TC should not have a transformer or electrical panel located in the space or within ten feet of the cabinet location in an adjacent space.

By now, everyone has upgraded their buildings for data networks where they have created locations for technology even though those buildings were not designed with technology in mind. Even in those older buildings, the simple rules stated above apply as best as possible. Fortunately, most systems are moving to the data network and with wireless networking becoming the preferred way to connect computing devices, these rooms are becoming smaller. The existing locations will most likely work just fine for future years.

Assessment Questions Associated with the "Facilities" Silo:

- Is the district planning to construct any new facilities?
- New—are those facilities planning for a combination of flexible spaces for small student groups and collaboration areas in addition to standard learning spaces?
- New—is the district varying the designs for different grade levels?
- New—is the district planning for a "teaching wall" or "presentation surface?"
- New—is the district planning furniture purchases sized to a range of students, or one size fits all?
- New—is the district planning furniture purchases that allow students to reconfigure the space to match the student experience planned by the teacher?
- Is the district planning to renovate existing facilities?
- Renovate—is the district planning to revise the floor plan for a combination of flexible spaces for small student groups and collaboration areas?
- Renovate—is the district planning to remove existing marker boards and create a presentation surface?
- Renovate—did the district include replacing existing furniture with flexible furniture in the budget?
- If not, provide a grouping and summation of existing facilities.
- For existing facilities, provide an overview and summation of issues to be resolved regarding creation of a presentation surface.
- Provide a summation of how the district intends to create "assessment" classrooms that flex during the annual assessment period.
- Provide a summation of how the district utilizes media centers in the district. Are they research and reference spaces, project spaces, a combination, or something different?
- Provide an assessment of spatial relationships for most facilities in the district.
- Assess and group the TR and TC spaces in district facilities.
- Outline any deficiencies with regard to the ANSI/TIA/EIA standards.

NOTE

1. George H. Copa (University of Minnesota, College of Education) and Virginia H. Pease (University of California at Berkley), "New Design for the Comprehensive High School" (Berkeley, CA: National Center for Research in Vocational Education—UC Berkeley, 1992).

Chapter 8

The Hidden Support Systems

The best practices herein are a compilation of various sources. Those sources include best practices for educational facility design as documented in various white papers, presentations, and guidelines from the Council of Educational Facility Planners International (CEFPI. org); the U.S. Environmental Protection Agency (EPA) and their Indoor Air Quality (IAQ) standards as required by various building codes and practiced by the construction industry. It also outlines the internationally and ANSI recognized TIA/EIA standards for data cabling and the spaces where the cabling is terminated and data network hardware lives. It also includes best practices as observed by the author from various school districts, educational planners, and architects.

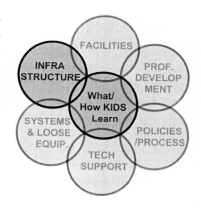

This silo is the most straightforward of all to address regarding issues within the silo affecting student-centered twenty-first-century learning and teaching. There are some issues that vary dependent upon which part of the United States your facilities are located in but overall, the issues are answered with a yes or no response: simple. The word "infrastructure" means many things to many different people. Within the context of school facilities, we are restricting ourselves to HVAC, AC power, and cable pathways.

HEATING VENTILATION AND
AIR-CONDITIONING SYSTEMS (HVAC)

We will first address the needs of the instructional spaces by simply pointing out the current IAQ standards as addressed by the EPA and integrated into building codes are radically different from when your older facilities were constructed. If you are constructing a new facility or your renovation project includes replacement of existing HVAC systems, your architect and mechanical consultant will provide a system that adheres to the current standards and there is nothing we can add to the conversation.

Older facilities are a different set of issues altogether. For those of you who have converted an old classroom into a computer lab, you know what I mean. What many readers may not understand is that the current standards expect a certain mix of fresh air with internal conditioned air along with a function that what is called "air exchange." Air exchange means that the space has enough air flow that the old air is exchanged for new air on a predictable rate.

Older systems were not designed to reach the air exchange rate of the new systems. Back to the classroom converted into a computer lab. Those of you with those rooms know that when you walk into one of those spaces around 1 p.m., all you want to do is fall asleep. The primary reason is that with a low air-exchange rate, carbon dioxide builds up in the room, which in turn causes drowsiness.

The other factor is that the room will get warmer as the day goes on due to the fact that you have added as many desktop computers as students. A desktop computer with old cathode ray tube (CRT) will generate almost as much heat per hour as a human body (liquid crystal display [LCD] screens drop the output to two-thirds of that total). Not only is the HVAC system not able to keep up with the carbon dioxide content, the system was not designed to handle the heat load of human bodies plus computers. So now you have an overly warm space with high carbon dioxide content. No wonder people get drowsy.

Unfortunately, this happens in older standard classroom spaces also as the facility HVAC system loses efficiency. An environment that causes people to feel drowsy is not very conducive to learning. HVAC systems can have an impact on student-centered twenty-first-century learning and teaching.

Another factor in older classroom spaces is noise. As correctly documented by the Acoustical Society of America (ASA), the older, self-contained HVAC systems, window units, or in-wall systems create more noise as they age. That noise becomes a major hindrance to communications within the instructional space. It can even lead to teachers being tired after a day of class because they had to raise their voices above the level of the noise for the students hear them. If there are hindrances to voice communications in a classroom, there is a hindrance to learning. Unfortunately, the only solution to the noise problem is new HVAC systems.

The other spaces impacted by HVAC systems are your technology spaces, the Telecommunication Room (TR) and Telecommunication Closet (TC). With regard to your TR, they generate enough heat that they must have good circulation year-round regardless of where in the country your facilities are located. I will state that Google has determined from their massive computing centers that the electronics can withstand much more heat than anyone thought. They keep the front of the cabinet in the nineties and the exhaust stack on the rear of the cabinet in the one hundred and twenties.

That means you do not have to cool the TR down to below seventy degrees. As long as you have good air exchange, minimum six times per hour, and the cabinets have exhaust fans, the room can stay in the high eighties. When your mechanical engineer really looks at the situation, it is really more about exhausting hot air than cooling the room down. Eighty degrees is warmer than any conditioned space surrounding the TR, even in the winter. Unfortunately, the ANSI/TIA/EIA standards have not yet incorporated Google's findings into their standards.

Cooling TRs in older buildings can raise some interesting issues. Most of the time, utilization of cooling systems that are called "split systems" represents the least expensive method for providing the proper air-conditioning for those spaces.

The TC spaces represent a different set of requirements with fewer concerns about the environment. Typically, the TC contains only network switches and cable terminations. Obviously, unless the wiring is submerged in water, there is little the environment can do to affect the performance of the cabling. The network hardware does not have any storage systems, only electronics, and it can withstand temperatures higher than a server.

However, there are limits. As long as the cabinet is in the building and the fans are properly exhausting hot air someplace other than the closet, you do not need to provide special conditioned air for those spaces. The primary concern is simply airflow/air exchange.

This does not apply to older school facilities designed as "finger schools" located in the Deep South or southwest area of the United States. "Finger schools" are campuses where there are a series of buildings with classrooms built in a line, side by side, and whose classroom doors open directly to the outdoor environment. Those classrooms and the separate buildings are connected by walkways with canopies. In the Deep South, the problem is not simply temperature but also humidity.

Parts of the Southwest experience some really hot days. In both cases, the wiring cabinet needs to be located in a conditioned space. It is not unusual for those types of campuses to have a wall-mounted wiring cabinet in one of the classrooms in each building.

AC POWER (INSTRUCTIONAL SPACE)

This is one category that has changed radically in less than twenty years. When we first started wiring schools with networks and placing computers in the classrooms, the computers were such power hogs that placing two of the units in a classroom would trip the circuit breaker. We started piling in more AC power circuits in each classroom and computer labs were chock full of power. Then there was a concern about "isolated ground" circuits and, a little later, concerns about the size of the circuit neutrals because of the odd harmonic feedback caused by the new digital switching power supplies used in computing devices. Things swung from simple to really complex within a ten-year span of time.

The pendulum has now swung back the other way. The AC power requirements of web-browser-based tablets and Chromebooks/netbooks are approximately 10 percent of today's low-energy desktop computing devices with LCD display. Even in a six-hundred-student elementary facility where every student and teacher has a computing device, we can recharge all of those devices with the power we installed in a computer lab only five years ago. Our power needs do not end with recharging those devices, but the difference in power requirements are dramatic.

When we talk about today's student and teacher devices, the AC power need is more related to how we enable recharging the device's battery in the classroom. A three-year-old student device will provide only half of its original charge, providing half of the original time it can be used without recharging. Until battery technology improves, we must plan for recharging of student devices in the classroom. Readers should understand I am not suggesting power would be provided at student desks. There simply should be methods for recharging student devices in classrooms.

Tablets are relatively easy; there are multiport USB power stations available from multiple manufacturers. Just plug them into an outlet and leave them on top of a counter or piece of furniture. The students will need to have the USB cable required for recharging or perhaps a few are left in each space.

Chromebooks/netbooks are a bit more complicated in that their power supplies are not universal like a USB power plug (well, Apple tablets' USB power plugs are not universal with the rest of the world's USB products). Those computing devices come with a power supply. If all of your students have devices, you would only need a few in each classroom for those students who forgot their power changers and did not charge their device at home last night. You would also need some type of multioutlet strip for students to plug in their power chargers. If you have a set number of student devices in the classroom and more in mobile carts located in the collaboration space, then you would need power supplies in the classroom and with the mobile carts. There are a few Chromebook products out there that charge using USB.

The one other area where you will need to plan for extra AC power outlets are those special classrooms which you intend to use for online assessments. Not only do you need to plan for extra outlets in those spaces, the location of those outlets should be coordinated to align with the desks purchased for those rooms to create rows of testing desks. Additionally, it pays to place power extenders in the cable trays and perhaps even extra power supplies for student devices.

On a side note, we use the term "power extender," not multioutlet strip. Byrne Electrical Specialists out of Rockford, Missouri (www.byrne electrical.com) were able to get their products labeled by Underwriters Laboratory (UL) in a totally different category than simple multioutlet strips.

According to the National Electrical Code, you are not allowed to daisy-chain UL-listed multioutlet strips; that is, plug one into another. However, Byrne's plug-in electrical power extenders do not fall into the same UL category, which means you can plug one into another, creating a chain of power outlets in the cable trays of the rows of desks used for assessments.

AC POWER (TECHNICAL SPACES)

When it comes to power for technical spaces, you do need to pay attention to all of the complex issues we used for design parameters a while back. They are not as critical for TC locations where you only house data switches, but they are critical for the TR where your fileservers and Internet-access devices live. The ANSI/TI/EIA standards have very clear expectations regarding power and proper grounding. Your architectural team should be well versed in what those rooms require.

Your primary service devices—servers, storage systems, routers and core network switches—are becoming more complex and need to be handled with tender loving care when it comes to AC power. One of the primary things you must provide is battery backup through UPS Uninterruptible Power System (UPS) units. There are a number of online calculators that your IT department can use to determine the capacity of the UPS units required based on the quantity and type of devices in your TR.

Additionally, those UPS units must be connected to the network so an alarm can be triggered and the servers and storage systems shut themselves down in an orderly manner when power problems occur. Your IT department should have written a script that is triggered when the UPS unit hits a certain point of no return regarding AC power. That script tells each respective server or storage system the specific steps it must go through before turning off its own power.

If no one has told you, simply turning off a server that is running a database or while a storage system is being accessed can damage the database or storage systems and render them unusable. Shutting down a server or storage system by simply turning off the power, without the proper cautionary steps, is called a "cold shutdown."

The UPS units are in addition to any backup power generator located at the campus. Having a backup generator does not eliminate the need for UPS units in the TR. Even if you have a backup generator on campus and you lose AC power from your local power utility, it takes a while for the generator to start and deliver a stable AC power source. In the meantime, your servers, storage systems, and core switch have gone through a cold shutdown, potentially harming the data on those devices. So the UPS units provide the bridging AC power while the campus power generator comes online.

Another item that no one may have told you about: the types of incidents that cause file servers to shut down versus what tells your backup generator to run may have nothing to do with each other. A sustained drop in voltage will not cause your lights to go out, but that same drop in voltage will make the fileserver think it is supposed to simply turn off. So the incident never triggers the startup of your backup power generator. Meanwhile, the batteries of the UPS units are being drained to make up the difference in voltage. If the voltage sag occurs for a couple of hours, the UPS batteries will drain, and all of your sensitive equipment will eventually experience a cold shutdown. We always want to avoid that type of shutdown.

CABLE PATHWAYS

Most readers are not aware that there is a standard for how cable pathways are installed in your facilities. I hate to get technical, but when we have standards you need to know they are there. Most people will not remember the specifics of this section but at least you have a reference for where to go when you are preparing for a conversation with your architects, engineers, or vendors. We will also provide a simplified synopsis of the key points from the electrical code and ANSI/TIA/EIA standards.

Specifically, the National Electrical Code (NFPA 70) has a few key points regarding cable pathways. The NFPA 70 itself has a number of articles (section titles) addressing pathways for what are defined as Class 2 or Class 3 cables (standard 110V AC power is Class 1). Additionally, the NFPA 70 has Article 800.24, which explicitly states that accepted industry practices for the installation of low-voltage cables are the ANSI/TIA/EIA-568.C and ANSI/TIA/EIA-569.B standards. The following provides a high-level, daily language overview of pathway requirements:

National Electrical Code (NFPA 70)

- Cable jacket must be rated for environment it is installed in. If in an "air plenum" space (using the ceiling space as a return air plenum), it must be plenum rated. If installed in conduit located under the building slab, it must be rated for indirect burial.
- Cables cannot use the structure of the building as direct support. You cannot hang cables on the structural trusses of the facility.
- Cables cannot use components of another trade as direct support. You cannot use plumbing pipes or HVAC systems as support of cables.
- Anything used as a cable pathway—cable tray, ladder tray, conduit, J-hooks, surface mount raceway, and so on—must be suspended from or attached directly to the building structure. The pathway cannot be suspended from any other trade suspension point, pipe, ductwork, and so on.
- Cables cannot lie on the ceiling; they must be suspended above the ceiling.
- Abandoned cables (those no longer in use) must be removed from the structure.
- You cannot use the suspended acoustical ceiling grid cables as support for cables.
- If a cable pathway is located in an inaccessible area—drywall ceiling above a lobby or entrance—that pathway must be a conduit running from an open area on one side of the inaccessible area to an open area on the other side of the inaccessible area.
- Conduit stubs must have bushings over the end of the conduit, eliminating sharp edges that cut cable jackets and wires.
- Pathway penetration of firewalls must be made using metal conduit, size and quantity determined by 40 percent fill calculation of NFPA 70. After installation of cables, the conduit must be filled with ATSM-rated fire-stop material. It is recommended that you use what is called

"intumescent" fire-stop material. It is putty in a bag that expands when exposed to a specific temperature level or higher.

ANSI/TIA/EIA Standards

- All cables not installed in cable trays or conduit must be supported every forty-eight to sixty inches with supports tied to the building structure.
- Cables are to be installed in a neat and orderly manner (no rat's nests above the ceiling).
- Conduits for communications cables may not be less than three-quarter inches in diameter (¾"). Half-inch conduit is not allowed.
- All wall boxes are to be two-gang, extra deep (2⅞") boxes. You may use one-gang reducer plates where only a single gang plate is required.
- Conduits containing communication cables may not have more than 360 degrees (360°) of turns without the installation of a pull box.
- Interior conduits containing communication cables may not be longer than 150 feet (150') without the installation of a pull box.
- NFPA 70 Article 800-40 requires the electrical contractor to provide and install a "Telecommunications Grounding System," separate from the electrical grounding system, in accordance with ANSI/TIA/EIA-607.

Best Practice

- For those facilities built on the southern or eastern seaboards where medium to high humidity is a typical condition, there is one issue not addressed in any of the standards. When you have a return air plenum and floor pockets in the building slab (on grade), the conduit runs from the floor pocket, under the slab (in the earth) and back up into the building, terminating in the return air plenum space. That means there is a pressure differential between the space where the floor pocket is located and the return air plenum space.

What that really means is that conditioned air with a fair amount of humidity is being sucked into the floor pocket, through the buried conduit and into the air plenum space. The temperature in the buried conduit is substantially lower than the conditioned air being pulled in, which then causes condensation and the conduit will fill up with water. Since the cable is ending up in the air return plenum, it must be a plenum-rated jacket.

Guess what? The plenum cable jacket acts like a sponge, swelling to two times its normal size, and now you have water surrounding your copper cable conductors. In turn, that water degrades the copper and soon your cable is not performing to expectations or stops working altogether. The best solution we have found is:

- Blow out the water from the conduit.
- Install gel-filled communication cables rated for direct burial.
- As soon as the cable exits into the return air plenum, use a plenum-rated biscuit (a small splicing box) and convert to a plenum-rated jacket cable.
- After installing the cable(s), seal the return air plenum end of the conduit with waterproof silicone caulking. That stops the conditioned air from being pulled into the conduit and stops the condensation problem.

An interesting point about most of the information listed above is that while it is part of the NFPA 70, the majority of local jurisdictions (local building inspectors) are only aware of and enforce a few items. They will typically catch and enforce requirements regarding firewall penetrations, inaccessible ceilings, and cable jacket ratings. The inspectors have not been educated on the changes in the code. In turn, that means the general contractor and electrical contractor are aware of only those items the electrical inspectors enforce.

Not only do your specifications and drawings from the architect/engineer team need to address these pathway issues, someone from that team must inspect the electrical rough-in work to make sure it matches the specification and drawing requirements.

LIGHTING

There are two categories of lighting in classrooms we need to discuss: standard lighting-fixture systems and natural daylight. Decades ago, the intent with school lighting fixtures was to scatter as much light as far as possible. The old-style acrylic lenses on fluorescent fixtures are intentionally designed to scatter light out eighty-five degrees to each side of vertical. Those older fixtures light up the wall as much as the floor. While that makes the room seem brighter, it does not work well with projector images. Those older fixtures and lenses also produce a high amount of glare, which can be uncomfortable when trying to use computing devices and any type of flat screen display.

The more contemporary fixtures use parabolic lenses, which focus the light down, not scattering off the walls. They also do not cause the amount of glare the older lenses do. It is also part of the newer building codes that at least half of the lighting fixtures must be able to be turned off. A very simple solution is to have the electrical designer turn off the row of light fixtures closest to the projection surface when designing the 50 percent load change.

It is also important to note that the telecommunication rooms (TRs) and closets (TCs), the technical spaces, should have a minimum of 500lx (fifty footcandles) of light when measured one meter from the floor. That is part of the ANSI/TIA/EIA standards. Those lighting requirements apply to the front and the rear of the cabinets.

There is a tremendous amount of research that documents the positive impact natural daylight has on students. It is not a question of whether you should or shouldn't. A good daylight designer will tell you that you can have too much natural daylight and will control it appropriately. With regard to projector images, the issue today is "Where and how much?" Yes, we have projectors that can provide sufficient light output that the image is not washed out by natural daylight, but we cannot afford to install them in every classroom.

It is critically important that your design team provides an estimate of how much natural daylight will fall on the projection surface of your classroom. Your AV consultant should be able to calculate whether the light level is low enough. It would also be beneficial that your daylight calculations should be made for both the summer and winter months. The sun is on a much lower azimuth and will penetrate deeper into rooms during the winter than any other season.

Assessment Questions Associated with the "Infrastructure" Silo:

- Has the HVAC system been designed to current indoor air quality standards from the EPA?
- Is the TR provided with conditioned air year-round?
- Do the TCs have sufficient air-exchange capacity?
- Are the HVAC systems noticeably loud in the instructional spaces?
- Is the district using web-browser computing devices or standard computers, and if computers, do they have sufficient AC power capacity?
- Has a properly designed telecommunications building ground system been provided for the TR and TCs?
- Does the TR have UPS capacity?
- If so, is it monitored? And if so, how is it monitored?
- Are cable pathways installed to NFPA 70 and ANSI/TIA/EIA standards?
- If not, how do they deviate from the standards?
- Are the typical lighting systems in classrooms designed to darken that area near the projection surface?
- Is the facility designed to enable day lighting? If so, is the installation of projection systems accommodated?

Chapter 9

Systems and
Loose Equipment

For this last silo we will be using the
ITIL, the ANSI/TIA/EIA standards, the
IEEE, and best practices as observed and
compiled from various school districts
around the county.

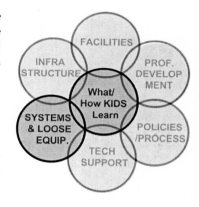

STUDENT COMPUTING DEVICES

First of all, student-centered twenty-first-
century learning and teaching requires
computing devices in student hands. The
student-centered learning environment
described in chapter 3 requiring formative assessments and the digital
tools enabling teachers to facilitate the process described in chapter 4
require student computing devices being available when and where the
students need them based on the student experience facilitated by the
teacher. A few devices in each classrooms and a couple of computer labs
in the building will not enable us to create the learning environment we
need to create.

Additionally, student and teacher devices are heading in a very specific
direction. An oversimplistic statement is that they should be web-browser
devices.

There are very few technologies we use that were designed for the
education market. Other than sound-field-enhancement systems, there
is virtually nothing we use in schools that has been designed and

manufactured specifically for use in schools. We can go back to the over-head projector as an example. In the mid-1940s, it was a closely guarded secret used by the military to project images of troop movements instead of moving pieces around on a big painted board as World War II was winding down.

Then in the late 1950s, they became the dominant way to display your score at the local bowling alley. Not too long after that, in the early 1960s, the federal government provided a large number of grants for technology in schools and everyone in schools started purchasing overhead projectors. They have been a dominant display technology in schools until the early 2000s. Were they designed for schools? Obviously not.

We must look outside of the education market to understand where technology is heading. When we look at current technology, touch-sensitive smartphones and tablets have taken over the industry. Those devices use web-browser technology to provide their higher-order functions. When we take a hard look at what the majority of students need to meet their learning experience, it is not a desktop or laptop device, it is a web-browser-based device.

As outlined in chapter 5, those devices need to cost less than $300 each or the funding mechanism will not work. There are no new sources of revenue available to schools anywhere in the next five to ten years, so to meet our "efficiency" goals of technology purchases we have to fit our computing-device purchases into the existing financial structure. That has implications for a number of areas.

These web-browser-based devices have a huge impact on efficiency. As an example: an assessment was conducted of a district prior to facilitating development of a Creating a Culture of Learning Plan with Roadmap. They had two computers at the rear of every classroom located in their elementary schools. When asked what the computers were used for, the teachers explained that they have a large percentage of elementary students with poor reading skills. They placed two computers with a self-paced reading literacy program in each classroom to enable access for those students needing development on a daily basis.

An observation was that the program they were using could run as a PDF, which means any inexpensive tablet or netbook would fill the bill. In comparison, the cost for two computer workstations was equal to four wireless netbooks, Chromebooks, or smaller tablets. By moving to a web-browser-based device, the school would increase its productivity impact by 100 percent, impacting four students in each elementary classroom at a time rather than two. When you add the costs for desks, chairs, hard-wired data port, and data ports in the closet versus wireless, it slants the productivity factor even higher.

The second area of efficiency gained by using web-browser devices is in computing-device technical support. There are no applications to update and support, or files stored on those devices. The applications and files live out in the public cloud where the people running the applications and storing the files handle the threat management (antivirus, security patches, etc.) and software updates. Additionally, if the applications and files live out in the public cloud, there is very little your technical support people need to do to support them. Yes, there are considerations regarding the bandwidth available from your building to the Internet, and we will address those in the section on networks.

A third area of efficiency is that all of these smartphones, netbooks/ Chromebooks, or tablets are what we call "stateless" devices. The concept could be explained but most of you would wonder why it is important when it can be summed up this way: based on the number of lines of program/software code required to make these web-browser systems work, they are radically simpler than desktops and laptops. We all recognize that the more complex a system becomes, the greater the chance that failure will occur. How often has your smartphone simply stopped working other than when you dropped it? How often does your laptop or desktop simply stop working?

Hopefully you are starting to understand that your future student computing device is a netbook/Chromebook or tablet. A full-blown desktop or laptop being the most effective and efficient computing device for students is no longer a valid concept.

There are exceptions to that statement. Specifically, there are content areas in high schools where the student instructional activity requires a computer with a processor and storage on board; for example, Photoshop, AutoCAD, video/audio editing. In today's world your computers in those content-specific computer labs need to be standard desktop units. However, even your business/marketing computer labs and foreign language labs are on the cusp of going web-browser based, dependent more on the application you want to run and whether it has been upgraded to web-browser-based access.

An area requiring a little more finesse will be those applications utilized by your special-education department and their students. The traditional applications are Windows based and the respective vendors have essentially ignored innovations driven by the Apple iPhone and iPad, smartphones, and interactive tablets. A second set of vendors has moved into that gap, creating interactive tablet applications which cannot run on a Windows-based PC. If your special-education department is not looking outside the Windows computing applications environment, they will tell you they must have a PC to run their applications.

Those districts and their teachers who have made the shift to interactive applications for special education are very adamant that they will never go back to nonmobile computing devices with noninteractive display screens. When you stop and consider that today's one-year-old and two-year-old children clearly understand how to manipulate aspects of interactive displays yet they do not understand a mouse and a keyboard-control system, it becomes self-evident that an interactive display is a superior delivery system for those students with special needs. The task becomes one of assisting your special-education department with the transition.

There is another major factor we must discuss before we leave the overview of student computing devices. Whether your state has joined the PARCC or SBAC consortium or is doing its own thing, the new curriculums come into play for the 2014–2015 school year. That means online testing of your students to the new standard starts in the spring of 2015. Touch-sensitive tablets work very well and are very engaging.

However, the new assessments will require your students, starting with fifth-graders, to type answers to questions; they are not multiple choice. The ability to communicate and express yourself in written form is crucial in today's marketplace. The new assessments will attempt to quantify the writing skills of your students and assess higher-order thinking skills through typed answers.

The test will require your students to type the answers. That implies you will need to start developing student keyboarding skills in the third grade. Wait a minute! Keyboard? Have you attempted to type much of anything on a tablet? What a pain.

The second thing about the online tests is that your state will have some minimum screen-resolution and size requirements for the devices used by students during the test period. The smaller tablets will not meet that requirement. No one can afford to have student computing devices that are used only for online testing purposes in the spring. Those devices need to be ones students use throughout the year and are flexible, and your technology systems support staff can use the network log-in and authentication application to lock them down when they are used for the online test.

This is one statement that will date this book. At this time, there are no interactive tablets of sufficient screen resolution and size with the ability to interface a keyboard to them that cost $300 or less. Tablets seem appropriate for PreK through second grade but starting with third-graders, most districts will end up with netbooks or Chromebooks.

TEACHER DEVICES

This book consistently states that the tools your students and teachers use should be migrating away from the old client/server model to a more contemporary model of using the web browser for connections and access. When you use an application that requires the client/server model, there is a small bit of the application software living on the teacher laptop or desktop. When the teacher launches the application, that software connects to the server and they talk to each other. It guarantees that the user computing device could access the full functions of the application located on the server. This model of computing was created long before the web browser came into being.

Managing both the server and the remote client side of the application can be full of complications. When things get complicated, they will fail more often. When your IT department only has to manage the server and the user connects using a web browser, there are fewer things that can go wrong. Simply stated, there are fewer interruptions of service to the user when using a more modern web-browser method. It is much more efficient to connect using a web browser than a client/server application.

So if your teacher tools are web-browser-based and the documents your students use for homework are web-browser based, is there some overriding need to give your teacher a full-blown desktop or laptop computer? There are none. Actually, the same straightforward netbook or Chromebook you are using for your students will meet the needs of most of your teachers.

There are a few teachers in the upper grades where the content and learning style of the classroom lends itself to the teacher using annotation with their demonstrations or examples. At that point, it seems reasonable to provide those teachers with a touch tablet (or pen tablet) with a ten-inch screen and a Bluetooth keyboard built into the cover.

DATA NETWORKS

It was not that long ago that we installed daisy-chain Ethernet and IBM Token-Ring data networks. The industry has come a very long way in developing hardware and control logic for very high-speed networks. Medium-priced hardware will have virtually all of the functions and protocols you need to manage your data network in a way that enables reliable and high-speed connections. We discussed the need for your staff to have skill sets equal to your needs, or, at worst, the ability to hire external augmentation services to set up your network in chapter 6.

The number of school buildings out there with outdated cabling and hardware is decreasing each year. However, there is one primary issue you need to understand, and it is a concept with the acronym VLAN (virtual local area network). In the early days of hardwired data networks the only way we could ensure that the data traffic from one set of computers was not seen by another set of computers was to create two separate physical networks. Each set of computers would have its own cabling, network hardware, and servers. Or perhaps the connection to the server was through a router (think a really fast-moving traffic cop).

Today's hardware, and the firmware (software burned on to a chip), allows us to create separate networks using logic rather than physical connections, and that is what we term a VLAN. Your technology system support team can set up your network in a manner where the communications from one set of computing device (i.e., teachers) is never seen by other computing devices (i.e., students) even though they all connect across the same set of physical wires and data hardware.

Your technology systems support team members need some deep skill sets regarding VLANs and data-traffic prioritization protocols to enable today's twenty-first-century learning environment. If they do not have them, find a consultant who will set up your networks and train the technology systems support team on what they need to know to keep the systems operating and place that consultant on a retainer or service contract.

Today's twenty-first-century learning environment literally requires high-density wireless networking. If your technology systems support team says it can't be done reliably, ask them "Then how does X University/College a few miles from here enable students to have two or three devices operating in one classroom?" Higher education has solved the high-density wireless problem and there is no reason why the K–12 industry cannot follow their example.

It would be of value for readers to understand that not all manufacturers of wireless network hardware are equal. In general terms, there are three types of systems out there. The simplest are those stand-alone wireless access points we use in our homes. They cannot deliver a high-density wireless environment.

The second level of systems is those where the wireless access points, the units installed throughout your building, are controlled by a centralized controller unit. There are good things that these systems do but you only need to know what they do not do well. The problem is that the controller must actually process every bit of data transmitted through the network.

As an example, there are two wireless computing devices in a classroom. When one device sends data to the other device, it is not a direct connection. The data first goes to the wireless access point, across the network to the centralized controller, back from the centralized controller to the same access point and then to the other computing device. The centralizer controller is the chokepoint.

Unfortunately, no one has been able to create a centralized wireless controller with sufficient bandwidth and processor speed to handle the amount of traffic caused by each student having a wireless device (much less the higher education need to service multiple devices per student). Adding more centralized controllers move the costs of these systems way beyond what a school district will spend for a high-density wireless network that actually works.

The type of system capable of delivering high-density wireless networks does have a central controller but the controller does not manage the network traffic. The controller manages the operational parameters of the access points, including which channels are activated and how strong of a signal should be used on that channel. The controller can be located in your buildings or out on the Internet, "in the cloud." These controllers can manage thousands of access points, not the hundreds of the system outlined in the previous paragraph. What makes these systems work for high-density wireless access is that the network traffic is handled by the individual wireless access point.

Each access point has chips on board with algorithms that manage the wireless traffic for those wireless devices connected to the access point. By pushing the traffic management out to the edge of the network, the network can handle a very high volume of traffic. This is similar to the technology used to manage the cellular phone networks across the United States. It is important to understand this type of system because not all of the major manufacturers have systems based on this technology.

You need to ask your vendor where the traffic for your wireless network is managed. Is it at the controller or at the individual access point? You want the traffic controlled at the individual access point.

Those of you who have the second level of wireless systems with a centralized controller, we have pointed out your controller will need to be replaced. Unfortunately, your existing wireless access points will not work with the new systems and they will need to be replaced also. The other major thing to understand about the new products is that the intelligent wireless access points will only work with a controller from the same manufacturer. Every company uses a different set of software and hardware.

However, the good news is that high-density wireless networking is here and works very reliably. There is no reason that your district should not start to adopt one of these new networks. The other good news is that for any facility you build from the point you start adopting one of the systems, the requirements for hardwired data ports will be drastically reduced.

Before leaving the data network section we need to explore the impact of moving to cloud-based documents and digital content and your Internet connectivity. Even when we are talking about the chapter 3 "digital learning" with fewer computing devices than "digital content," moving to cloud-based resources may have a detrimental impact on the response

time of your Internet access. Obviously, as the student population becomes larger, the required access speed will become larger.

K–12 school organizations have a much tougher problem regarding Internet access when compared to universities/colleges, private and public
companies, or individual users accessing from home. There are multiple
federal laws and regulations regarding the Internet and safety for minors.
That forces your technology systems support team to provide content fil-
tering and control methodologies for all of your Internet access. In turn,
that requires all of your Internet connections to come through a single
point with all of your facilities connecting back to that one point.

So as your Internet access needs increase, you must increase the bandwidth of your direct connection to the Internet and the circuits connecting
your campuses back to that one point. Speaking frankly, that will be a
really expensive proposition. The cost for internal connections between
campuses is a major hindrance to all school districts.

There are alternative ways to increase your Internet access without
actually increasing your access bandwidth. You can place or create an appliance (a server with an application) for "web caching." A "web cache"
appliance will analyze, or you can program the device to analyze, the
places your users go on the Internet on a regular basis. During hours
when your Internet-user access is not heavy, it will go to that location and
download the most recent webpage or video and store the information on
its hard drives. Then when a user clicks on the webpage, the request actually goes to the web cache and the user receives the most recent webpage
from the appliance.

That eliminates the user request from actually going out to the Internet
and using up your available bandwidth. It may be of value to note that
the locations accessed by elementary students are different than those for
middle schools and yet different again for high-school students. It may
be of value to create different web cache appliances for different grade
levels or even content areas, dependent on how many students are in
your school district.

The second alternative is related to when you move to one of the cloud-
based office suites. You place another appliance either at the school level
or for a cluster of campuses that acts as the cloud storage system. It works
the same way as the web-caching appliance. When the Internet access us-
age is low, it goes out to the cloud and aligns what students and teachers
have stored on the appliance with what is stored on the cloud.

It again eliminates or substantially reduces the need for real-time access
to the Internet. Both of these alternate solutions are a realistic path for
most districts when every student has a computing device.

SERVERS

There is a word your technology support people should have mentioned and educated you on as to what it means: *virtualization*. Server virtualization is a fairly simple concept. You first inventory each application running on your servers (e-mail, SIMS, etc.) and how much of the resources for each server the application is using. Server resources are the CPU capacity, RAM memory capacity, input/output capacity, and storage capacity of the server (box).

You then purchase a larger capacity, more robust, less-susceptible-to-failure server and create what are called virtual servers on that one box. You then install an application on that virtual server but the entire server box will run multiple applications instead of one application per server. If your e-mail application uses only 10 percent of the server box it is installed on, that is a very inefficient use of that server. It also costs less to purchase a higher-capacity server that runs multiple applications and has more features that prevent loss of service than those multiple servers.

Some examples: District A reduced the number of server boxes at the district office and in each building from 480 down to ninety boxes. District B reduced the servers at the district office from fifty-eight boxes down to four boxes. If you have not already done so, your district should be working on your server-virtualization program.

Even though they are not technically servers, your storage systems have become much more important. You are running applications with some powerful databases and those databases require an absolutely stable and robust storage system. There are also federally mandated requirements regarding archiving of e-mail and social-media applications used by the district. When we add federal laws regarding child safety and the Internet, social-media applications used for learning cannot be the public systems your students use when they are away from campus.

Network storage for teachers and students is another really large issue. Teachers hate to change their habits and store their files on the network (your storage system) but it is an extremely important change they need to adopt. However, your actual storage requirements will go down dramatically in the near future. That statement is driven from the viewpoint that your district will migrate to one of the cloud-based office applications—the free Google Docs or ZOHO Office (Linux based), or Microsoft's Office 365, which is a free application but cloud storage (the purpose for using it) has some costs.

The point is that your students' and teachers' files will be stored in the cloud, and there will be no need to store or back them up on your system. Current levels are fifty GB of storage for free for every user.

Let's put that in perspective. If you have three thousand students, two hundred teachers, and another one hundred administrators, you will receive 165TB (terabytes) of storage. Not only is it storage, it is basically fault-tolerant storage. It would cost $40,000 for you to purchase what we call Network Attached Storage configured in RAID5. Then there would be quite a bit of time for your IT department to set it up and keep it running. If you want for really fault-tolerant storage similar to what the office suite people are using, it would run around $300,000.

VOICE COMMUNICATION SYSTEMS

How people communicate via voice between each other on one campus, from one campus to other district facilities, or from the district to places outside the district has no real impact on student academic achievement. However, from an administrative and business-of-education viewpoint, voice communications are a necessity. They are also fairly straightforward in how they are actually used.

We need to talk about two different systems. We have the traditional internal communication system for schools in the form of two-way, hands-free intercom systems. The other system is a VoIP phone system running on the data network.

There is a bit of disconnect with the rationale of providing both a two-way intercom and a VoIP phone in the classroom. What is the logic behind providing two separate voice communication channels to each classroom? Today's two-way intercom system with ceiling speakers and a handset in the classroom is a very poorly designed phone system with few system features available on a standard VoIP system.

To help readers understand, let's take a different look at that concept. Who do you think puts more research and development and quality control into the manufacturing of their systems, the intercom manufacturer who sells $10 million in intercoms per year or the phone manufacturer who sells $1 billion in phone systems? The research and development budget of the $1 billion phone-system manufacturer exceeds the total sales of the intercom manufacturer.

That is not to suggest that schools do not need some type of building-wide voice announcement system (one-way paging). In fact, the last two new fire code publications (NFPA 72) have a complete new chapter focusing on voice announcement systems. They are one leg of that the new fire code calls MNEC (Mass Notification and Emergency Communication systems).

In the near future your local building code jurisdiction will be educated on the new codes and it will require one of those systems in any new building or building addition your district constructs. Your older buildings without MNEC systems will be grandfathered into the new code without requiring upgrades until you do major renovations in the building.

However, those systems are one-way, building-wide announcement systems with battery backup, enabling them to work even when the campus loses AC power. There are some other technical issues around how the system actually monitors and confirms that the speaker are working, which none of today's intercom systems are capable of doing. Those systems will also require UL certification that they meet the monitoring functions.

With the limited revenue stream from existing intercom system sales, I do not expect any of the existing intercom manufacturers to be financially capable of reengineering their intercom systems to meet the MNEC requirements and obtain the appropriate UL certification.

As noted a few paragraphs ago, there are features available with VoIP systems that are not available with intercom systems. Part of the typical bias against intercoms is lack of a voicemail system that conforms to current united messaging standards. Those are the standards that enable you to receive a voicemail via e-mail or text or generate a text message using your voice on your smartphone. Those capacities were actually developed for VoIP phone systems and were adapted to the smartphone environment. Two-way intercom systems simply do not have those features.

The second feature is the software-based control capabilities of a VoIP phone system. You can program the extension for a classroom so that a call from the main office rings in the classroom yet a call from a phone external to the district is automatically sent to voicemail only during school hours. Part of that programmability makes the system more beneficial than a two-way intercom.

There are applications available that when a classroom phone uses the "distress code," the information about the distress code can be displayed on the phones of multiple administrators, office personnel, or security personnel simultaneously. There is no need for a central person to relay the information from the intercom system over to the personnel who need to know there is a "situation" in progress and they need to respond.

There is one potential negative factor about today's VoIP phone systems. We have VoIP phone sets that work on a wireless Wi-Fi network but they are prohibitively expensive. It is less expensive for the district to install a hardwired data port in the classroom and connect a hardwired VoIP phone handset than purchase one of those expensive wireless handsets. It may be of value to have a couple of those wireless handsets available for use at the bus loop, but the district needs to ensure that the Wi-Fi system extends to that area of the campus.

INSTRUCTIONAL TECHNOLOGIES

There is one last bias that we need to talk about and it relates to instructional technology. The dirty little secret no one every talks about is: "We have little idea of what does and does not work to increase academic achievement with regard to instructional technology." Other than the sound-field enhancement systems (infrared microphone system for teachers and students), we have no real data to work with.

We also have no data that one product works better than another product in the same category of technology. Granted, from learning research we know that audiovisual presentations work better than lecture or reading assignments, but beyond that, there is a complete dearth of information.

That is not to say it does not make sense to provide large-screen video projectors for communicating with digital natives who are more visual-spatial oriented than we are. It means we do not know to what degree it works better than other video-delivery systems. We only have anecdotal evidence. We make assumptions based on that anecdotal evidence.

It also appears that school districts tend to implement technology based on our teacher-centered historical viewpoint. We will take what we are familiar with and try to figure out how to adapt it to a student-centered environment. That adaptation may not be the best solution for a twenty-first-century student-centered learning environment.

Here are some basic parameters of video and how a student-centered viewpoint may provide a totally different solution than what we typically see in a classroom. There are a number of "rules of thumb" related to video and one of them is that when we want to see higher-resolution graphics, like the "Menu Bar" at the top of the screen of a computing device running Windows, the rule of thumb is: the screen height must be equal to one-sixth of the distance of the farthest viewer to the image.

When your students are sitting in orderly rows, the farthest person from the screen will be approximately twenty-two feet away. The height of your screen should be forty-four inches. Take a look at your marker boards and any larger interactive boards and you will find they are that size or slightly larger. Coincidence?

No, people simply prefer the larger board, which provides a larger image, because it seems most comfortable when trying to see an image from anywhere in the classroom. The "height of screen equals one-sixth of viewing distance" rule of thumb came into play. So the larger image is required so everyone can see the image from anywhere in the room.

Let's play with that basic concept and see what other configuration would work. We now have a modern classroom with flexible furniture. The teacher utilizes twenty-first-century learning methodologies that include students working in small collaborative groups. Let's say this is a high school and there are five groups of five students. The only time we would be using a wall-mounted projection system is when the teacher is directing the students regarding their next activity or a group of students are presenting their project.

Presentations are what we call a "One-to-Many" information transfer. Realistically, the amount of time where One-to-Many information transfer should be occurring in a twenty-first-century learning environment is much lower than the teacher-centered learning environment most students experience today. Providing a wall-mounted projector system and interactive tool may not be the most efficient use of my instructional technology funds.

Instead, let's provide a fifty-inch LCD flat-panel display on a mobile cart. The cart also has a computing device that connects wirelessly to the network and some type of interactive video tool that makes the display an interactive unit. That cart moves around the room (it only needs AC power), so a group of students can work on a project or presentation.

When the students make their presentation, the teacher says "Everyone else, drag your chairs over to the LCD cart." Or when used in the earlier grade-level classrooms, "Students, gather around and sit on the floor." A fifty-inch, wide-aspect-ratio flat panel will have a twenty-five-inch screen height. As long as all of the students are within twelve feet of the screen, they can see everything they would be seeing on a wall-mounted projector system.

We accomplish the same function of using video in a radically different way and the video is no longer tied to a specific location on the wall. Hopefully you picked up that flexible furniture is a key to the solution. These types of alternative viewpoints will be the more prevalent as more classrooms move to student-centered environments rather than teacher-centered environments. It would be of value to work through all of the instructional technologies we are installing in our classrooms.

SOUND-FIELD ENHANCEMENT SYSTEMS

If you have not been exposed to one of these systems, they are a combination of an infrared microphone system, audio mixer, audio amplifier, and speakers. The basic concept is that the teacher, or a student speaking to the class, uses an infrared microphone that is amplified through the sound system. That way the teacher or student making a presentation can be heard by everyone without being required to raise his or her voice level.

It is an important point that the microphone uses infrared light for connecting the microphone to the receiver. That means the signal of the microphone will not bleed from one room to the next. Light cannot penetrate walls. You can also connect the audio input from a computing device, tablet, or other source and it will amplify it across the system.

This is the easiest system to discuss in that this is the one system we do have data regarding how it impacts academic achievement. Across the years, there have been a number of studies (including controlled studies—comparing classes with the systems and classes without) that indicate that the implementation of a sound-field enhancement system has an impact of raising student test scores by 7 to 12 percent. If you have money for only one instructional technology system, this one system will do more for your students than anything else you can do.

INTERACTIVE WHITEBOARDS

This is one of the technologies used in classrooms where we have no data on whether it has an actual impact on academic achievement, positive or negative. However, this is a technology everyone considers as an indication that your district is implementing "current" technology concepts. Perhaps we are accepting a number of premises regarding the value of these systems that are simply not substantiated.

We assume that since interactive whiteboards have generated anecdotal evidence (stories) that students are more engaged when the teacher uses them in a twentieth-century teacher-centered environment, they would still be of value in a student-centered twenty-first-century learning environment. However, we have clear data that discussions, hands-on projects, and students teaching each other are the more efficient ways for people to retain knowledge.

If your learning environment emphasizes those types of activities, how much student time during the day should be spent receiving information from the teacher in presentation mode? Not a large percentage of their day. We need to answer the question, "Where in a student-centered twenty-first-century learning environment does an interactive whiteboard fit? What student-centered experiences are appropriately tied to that technology? How many students can use that technology at one time?"

Another question is how much of your limited revenue do you want to spend on technology that we hope does not get used a majority of the time in each learning day? There is little correlation between the value of an interactive whiteboard in a teacher-centered environment and the premise that it will have similar value in a twenty-first-century student-centered learning environment.

Taking a totally different train of thought, if you are one of those districts planning to provide every student with a device, why would you use an interactive whiteboard when every student can individually access the presentation? Whether the presentation is from a student or the teacher, each student could simply open the file on their device from the classroom "shared" location in the cloud and follow along. A typical response is; "As the teacher, I want to be able to see their eyes and be able to know that they are paying attention."

That is definitely a teacher-centered environment response. Are we not expected to use formative assessments to determine what our students did and did not learn today? Looking into someone's eyes to estimate if they are learning is a very subjective process, and basing tomorrow's student experience on an a subjective observation is an unsubstantiated viewpoint. There appears to be little support for the premise that we need a large-screen presentation system in a learning environment where every student has a device.

At this point your response may be, "I hear what you are saying, but we want it anyway because everyone else has them and our constituents expect to see them in the classroom." Or another one could be "I hear what you are saying but that is long way from where we are to today. We need to move our teachers to a digital learning environment before we move to a total digital content environment. Using interactive whiteboards as part of that transition will help our district in eventually making those big jumps." Both statements represent very valid rationales for using interactive whiteboards.

The reality of funding mechanisms around the country is that your constituents need to have the perception that you are doing what you can to properly educate students. If they perceive you are not doing well or are not properly focused, they will limit your access to funds. If your constituents expect to see interactive whiteboards in the classroom, you need to provide interactive surface capability.

We also need to help teachers make the transition to digital learning and eventually digital content environments. There is no data indicating using interactive whiteboards actually helps with the transition to student-centered learning. But again, if your teachers perceive it would, installing interactive capability may help you move forward with a more student-centered learning culture.

If you are a district in one of these categories, we need to explore what aspects of interactive whiteboards are of actual value to your learning environment. It is interesting to note there are fifteen different firms out there offering an interactive whiteboard product. Making a surface interactive is fairly simple with today's technology; actually, it's extremely simple and extremely inexpensive.

To see an example of how simple and inexpensive it can be, log onto YouTube and search for "Johnny Li and Wii Controller." While a student at Carnegie Mellon University, Johnny Li figured out that he could take a Wii controller and with $65 of parts turn any surface a projector could shine an image on into an interactive surface. Oh! So I do not need the actual board mounted on the wall.

If it is so simple and inexpensive to create an interactive surface, why are there at least fifteen companies offering interactive whiteboard products but only three of them are used in the K–12 environment? The answer is that the key element is not the interactive surface; all fifteen companies have that. The value those three firms bring to the K–12 marketplace is the large collection of applications (lesson plans/student experiences) generated by educators and available to other teachers who use that manufacturer's product.

So it is not the hardware that is unique, but the software. The hardware is actually fairly expensive to acquire and install. There are other ways to create an interactive presentation space in a classroom rather than purchasing and installing an actual interactive whiteboard. We need a projection surface and an interactive sensor.

There are multiple products that we can use as a projection surface. There are new versions of marker boards that do not create white-hot spots of glare when used with video projectors. There are projection and marker materials that can be glued to an existing marker board. A number of companies offer paint that enables the entire surface to be used as a marker board or projection surface. All of those can be used as the projection surface.

While we are on the subject of projection surfaces, we need to talk about the appropriate height of those surfaces. An interactive projection surface mounted at the same height as a marker board is problematic for at least PreK through second-grade students. If you want to make the projection surface interactive and reachable to those students, the image needs to be much closer to floor level. Eighteen inches above the floor seems to be a reasonable compromise height for early grade-level students and teachers. Special-education classrooms may need the image starting all the way down at floor level dependent upon the physical function level of the students.

There are multiple products available that you can use to make the projection surface interactive. A number of the projector manufacturers have seen the Johnny Li video and now offer interactive projectors. There are a couple of companies who make sensing units that you install at the edge of the area you want to be interactive and the surface becomes interactive. The three K–12 interactive whiteboard companies also have wireless slates that you work instead of using the projection surface.

Please keep in mind that the wireless slate does not work well for the early grade-level students either. We are just now starting to move to "gesture"-based controls. The gesture-based Microsoft Kinect unit used with the XBOX was hacked and then Microsoft released the control codes for the box. The Kinect can now control any Windows, Apple, or Chrome OS program using gestures. Phones and computers now have gesture-based control systems provided as a basic feature.

Once you have your projection surface and interactive sensor mechanism, you then pay a license fee and the interactive lesson plans/student experiences from one of the three K–12 interactive whiteboard companies can be used on your less expensive interactive surface. Well almost; not all of the K–12 providers of interactive whiteboards understand that the value of their products is their software. One company requires you to purchase a hardware product before you can purchase their software; it's silly but true.

VIDEO PROJECTORS

Now that we have a projection surface, interactive sensor, and applications, we need a projector to create the image we will interface with. There is little empirical data that indicates higher academic achievement when students do or do not have a large-screen projector in the classroom. On the other hand, we need to acknowledge that the higher-level skill sets in the CCS and communication skills for the twenty-first-century learner as outlined by P21.org imply that students need to know how to present information.

There are fewer questions regarding the value of a large image display (video projector or LCD display) when compared to the value of an interactive whiteboard. But again, if every student has a computing device, why can't the student presentation be brought up on all of the devices? Why would it have to be a large screen with everyone looking at me and the screen? Adults are typically more comfortable with a large-screen presentation but that may be an aspect of being a digital immigrant rather than a digital native.

Back to the subject at hand. Before we talk about projectors, we need to talk about projector location. When we first started installing projectors in classrooms, they were ceiling mounted and located ten or twelve feet from the projection surface. When the interactive boards started coming around, we found that the projector located that far away created a large area of shadow and the interactive part was not that easy. Using short-throw projectors located closer to the projection screen solves that problem.

One thing that we all need to understand is that the height of the projector from the floor is not supposed to be lower than eighty-four inches above the floor. The American Disabilities Act (ADA) comes into play when anything juts out more than four inches from a wall or hangs from a ceiling. So if we use a wall mount for the projector and the projector has a least thirty degrees of what we call "vertical keystone correction," we can mount the project or so it is not lower than eighty-four inches and still place the image down low for early grade-level students.

It may be of value to understand that the ultra-short-throw projectors mounted right on the wall do not have keystone correction, or very little if at all, and they will not enable you to move the image lower to the floor. On the other hand, you may be able to obtain an ADA waiver from the local jurisdiction that controls your building code and move the projectors lower and use ultra-short-throw projectors.

Regardless of where you install your projector, most of you are already aware of the basic needs like brightness, at least three thousand lumens and a contrast ratio of at least 1000:1. One thing you may not have heard is that the video graphics array (VGA) connection is essentially dead due to what is called the Analog Sunset Rule related to Blue-Ray DVD players and digital copy-protection methods.

They can enforce copying laws when you use HDMI connectors but not VGA. The new rule is that anything with a DVD player in it cannot have a VGA connection. The fact that you can stream Blue-Ray DVD signals to your computing device also eliminates the VGA connection from that computing device. So the projector you purchase today should have a dual-channel HDMI connection.

The second issue is a little more controversial in that it has additional costs related to the initial purchase; buy a projector with LEDs instead of bulbs. In today's market the projector would actually have blue and red LEDs with a green laser system. The expected life cycle of those lighting units is twenty thousand hours, or approximately twenty years of use. That means you no longer have to purchase replacement bulbs once every two years. Part of the extra cost is that most the projectors have the interactive control built in plus they have Ethernet and Wi-Fi connectivity.

Whether you connect the projector to your network or use some type of integrated AV system in the classroom, the main thing is you want to be able to set up a schedule where all projectors are automatically turned off at a certain time every day.

A case was made earlier that perhaps a large-screen LCD flat display on a mobile cart would work just as well as the projector. Let's review data shared back in chapter 1; PBL does not provide more effective academic growth because that delivery method does not work for the content area of mathematics.

Since PreK through fifth-grade classrooms typically teach math in the same classroom as all other content areas, either the large-screen LCD panel or projector is a necessity (not the interactive aspect). Once we move to grade levels where there are teachers who provide instruction in mathematics all day long and the district does not provide a device for every student, a large-screen projector is a necessity.

That also circles us back around to the "dirty little secret about technology in schools": we have no data that a single large display is superior or inferior to the same information on each student device.

INTEGRATED AV SYSTEMS

If you are connecting multiple devices to a projector system, we have need to make the control of the projector power and inputs and sound-system volume control a simple thing to control. Having some type of control system in the classroom now makes sense. Additionally, if that control system can talk to the network, then the help desk can look at the system while assisting the teacher and know exactly what the problem is. In this scenario, your projector is connected to the integrated AV system and all of your projector issues are handled through the control system web interface.

A number of the control system manufacturers now include the infrared microphone system as part of their integrated AV system. Additionally, there are major limits to how long an HDMI cable can be and these systems provide an HDMI extender, which converts all of the connecting cables to two or three CAT5 jumper cables. That makes it a very simple installation. There is nothing magical about these integrated AV systems; they are simply a matter of whether you are using a projector, and additional video sources and have the budget to accommodate the purchase and installation costs.

DOCUMENT CAMERAS

This is another one of the devices that are automatically added to a student-centered twenty-first-century learning environment but they come from a twentieth-century teacher-centered environment. If you stop and think about it, what physical object would a student have that he or she would need to place under a document camera? We are not saying that they do not have a place in specific content areas like science labs; they are an absolutely necessary tool for those content areas. We are simply stating that if students can access digital content and the Internet, what student experience would incorporate the use of a document camera?

This is another instructional technology device we use that does not have supporting data indicating it increases student academic achievement.

You may respond, "We can document a student project or a student needs to capture something for his or her student experience." We need to remember that in today's world all tablets, netbooks, and Chromebooks have a camera built into the computing device. Students can use the student computing device to document their project or creation. What is the value of a document camera in a twenty-first-century student-centered, PBL environment when students and teachers have computing devices with cameras?

PRESENTATION STATION

If you plan to use a wall-mounted video projector or mobile large-screen LCD panel in your instructional space, we have one more piece of technology to talk about, something called a "presentation station." Essentially it is nothing more than a desktop computer with an LCD screen, keyboard and mouse, running a current version of Windows, connected via HDMI to the large-screen display in the classroom. The desktop computer unit also connects to the local Wi-Fi network.

If you remember, all of the student and teacher computing devices use the Wi-Fi network. There are applications for all of those devices which enable us to "mirror" the student or teacher computing device screen on to a Windows desktop computing device. The applications use the local Wi-Fi connections to connect the student or teacher device to the desktop computing device. That means you can display the screen of the teacher or any student computing device on the large-screen display without moving the device or student. Everything happens across the Wi-Fi connection.

There is little that is twenty-first-century learning with regard to interactive whiteboards, large-screen projectors, and document cameras. They are advanced presentation tools emphasizing the "sage on stage" role of a primary information gatekeeper. The "advanced" classrooms we see as demonstrations where each group of students has their own large-screen display and each one can be seen by all of the other students in the space is well intentioned but still a presenter-focused basis. Once you work with three or four people on a truly collaborative enabled document (i.e., Google Docs) where what you do on your screen is immediately updated on the screen of the other collaborators, you will wonder why anyone would want to go back to the cumbersome use of a large screen and only one person enabled to make changes.

Creating a student-centered twenty-first-century learning and teaching instructional environment is not about using twentieth-century teacher-centered technology. It is about focusing on student-centered learning and rethinking what that means with regard to technology.

Assessment Questions Associated with the "Systems and Loose Equipment" Silo:

- What type of computing devices does the district use for student computers? Desktops computers, laptops, or netbook/Chromebook devices?
- What is the current ratio of devices to students?
- Does the district have plans to move to web-browser-based student computing?
- If so, what are those plans and have they assessed which of their current student applications must migrate to web-browser-enabled versions?
- What type of computing device does the district use for teacher computing?
- Does the district plan to move to web-browser-based teacher computing devices?
- If so, what are those plans and have they assessed which of their current applications must migrate to web-browser-enabled versions?
- Does the district use any of the cloud-based office applications?
- If the district has plans for students using cloud-based applications, how do they intend to ensure adequate access to the Internet and those applications?
- Does the district use VLANs on their data network?
- If yes, how have they set up the VLANs? (How many VLANs and what traffic is on which VLAN?)
- Does the district have any wireless networks?
- If so, are they using high-density wireless networks with intelligent access points?
- Does the district have standards regarding voice communication systems? If so what type of system have they standardized on?
- Is the district aware of the new NFPA 72 requirements for MNEC systems, and has it determined how it will address those new requirements?
- Does the district use sound-field enhancement systems?
- Has the district worked through twentieth- versus twenty-first-century aspects of interactive boards?
- Has the district standardized on an interactive manufacturer and methodology?

- Has the district standardized on projectors? LED/laser based?
- Has the district standardized on using an integrated AV system for classrooms? If so, what manufacturer have they standardized on?
- Has the district standardized on using document cameras? If so, what manufacturer has it standardized on?
- Has it considered using the teacher computing device (i.e., tablet) as a document camera?

Part II

THE PLANNING PROCESS AND DOCUMENTATION

Chapter 10

The Planning Process

Hopefully you now understand the complexity of the goal, creating a student-centered twenty-first-century learning and teaching culture in your district and the comprehensive nature of this planning process. As mentioned in chapter 2, one of the goals of this book is to provide sufficient information about the planning process for school districts that operate on limited budgets to possibly execute this planning process on their own. Part 1 provided a detailed look at the seven silos and their associated issues and observed best practices addressing those issues.

This portion of the book focuses on the tactical aspects of how to execute the planning process yourself or with minimal assistance. Chapter 11 addresses how to assemble the various findings into a usable document/report.

Those readers who are less interested in this aspect can read the next five pages for an overview of the planning process and then skip the remainder of this chapter and chapter 11.

OVERVIEW OF THE PLANNING PROCESS

Exposing the planning participants to the best practices, identifying district-specific hindrances and obstacles to student-centered learning in all silos, and generating goals and strategies addressing those hindrances and obstacles are at the heart of this planning process. This planning sequence, which develops an internal strategic plan, follows the sequence of the four questions in the diagram below for all seven of the silos contained within the coherent planning philosophy:

You start with the center silo of "What/How Students Learn" and work through each silo answering the three questions for each silo while reflecting on the instructional delivery/curriculum viewpoint.

Assessment—Where Are You Now?

The first step in the planning process is to assess the district's status within all seven silos against nationally recognized standards and best practices. Additionally, the facilitator(s) capture and account for all prior student-centered learning discussions and initiatives, which become the basis of this planning process. The diagram below outlines the seven silos with the pertinent standards and a list of the issues to be assessed in each silo. It should be noted that there are two assessment issues that cross all boundaries between the silos: communications and funding. The assessment requires on-site meetings with key district-level personnel, building-level personnel, inspection of a range of the existing facilities, regarding teaching activities in classrooms across a range of grade levels.

MET – EFFECTIVE LEARNING and TEACHING Assessment Overview

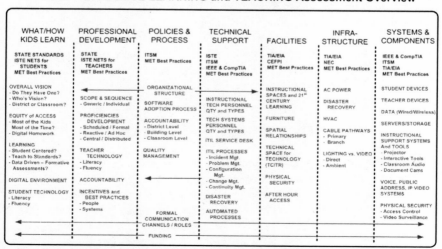

The assessment phase also includes data gathering regarding recent and current learning and teaching initiatives and state-level initiatives or directives that have an impact on the district. It also includes gathering historical information of past operating and capital budgets associated with teaching/learning and technology. Dependent on the planning parameters, it may include gathering data regarding current audiovisual and computing device inventory and facility inventory of spaces. The assessment phase is also designed to enable the planning facilitator to become familiar with the culture of the district prior to the start of the first planning lab.

Planning Lab 1—Where Do You Want to Go?

The next step of the plan is accomplished through a two-day planning lab where a complete representation of the organization members participates. It is extremely important that representatives from the policy level (superintendent, deputy and associate superintendents, perhaps board members), management level (principals), and classroom level collaborate together throughout the planning process. It should also include technologically oriented and nontechnologically oriented personnel. The process establishes common concepts and terminology similar to the introduction of this process and then moves to providing best practices as represented by current research and observations.

The participants are taken through a "Nominal Process" where they confirm the site-based observations and align their view of where the organization is with regard to "What/How Students" and "Professional Development" silos. During this planning session, the participants responses are tracked and key issues where the district does not align with best practices are identified, articulated, and prioritized. Participants' responses are also tracked with regard to their vision of what effective, efficient, and sustainable student-centered learning means.

When this planning process is aligned with a major construction initiative, the facilitator takes the participants through a process where they define the expectations regarding technology that should be implemented within every type of space located in the district. They discuss current trends and what is happening in the marketplace, and generate a graphical representation of the types of technology and quantities which the space should be capable of supporting. (This is creating an ideal implementation concept but it must be reconciled with available budgets.) This planning process should also integrate student participation in the design process right from the beginning as an effective student-centered learning tool.

Planning Lab 2—How Will You Get There?

The second planning session is where alignment of the plan to the cultural and political aspects of the local organization starts to come forward as the plan aligns to those realities. If the process is aligned with a construction initiative, the participants first review the lab 1 findings and participate in a second "Nominal" process that prioritizes the technologies described in the first planning lab. The participants then work in small groups on the prioritized issues and hindrances identified to refine the articulation of each individual issue, develop goals and strategies for accomplishing those goals, assign responsibility, and if possible provide a cost estimate to implement the strategy.

The planning participants will have worked on key concepts behind their vision for effective learning and worked those concepts into a Mission for Twenty-First-Century Learning and Teaching as part of their homework. The goal is to develop a statement from which a simple metric of what effective student-centered learning means. That metric becomes the dominant tool used at the district, building, and classroom levels to ascertain if each student experience represents an effective learning experience aligned with the goals of the organization.

The planning lab will also contain a reporting out of the capital and operational budgets available and start the process of reconciliation of funding requirements with available revenue. An overview of the timeline of the plan activities will also be reviewed. As a final activity, the planning participants will discuss and generate a set of metrics that will be used in five years to determine if the plan was successful. That should include explicit metrics matching the expectations of what is a reasonable set of goals to accomplish within the five-year term of the plan.

First Draft

The findings developed from the site-based assessment and two labs are to be assembled into a document that outlines the district's plan for "Creating a Culture of Learning." The document sequence of content follows the overall planning process flow. The first section will deal with the assessment of where the district is with regard to each of the seven areas of interest. The second section will provide definitions of where the district wants to go. The third section will outline how the district will get there—a roadmap. It includes goals and strategies addressing disconnects, roadblocks, and hindrances; goals and strategies related to implementation of new policies and processes; and reconciliation of revenue stream with prioritized implementation plans (operating and capital expenditures). This draft is forwarded to the cabinet and governing board.

Executive Cabinet/Board Review

Prior to the final plan review meeting, the facilitator will hold a web conference with the cabinet and governing board for feedback and discussion of the plan with the cabinet. The primary function of this activity is to ensure that the decision makers of the organization agree with and support the statements, strategies, and budgets contained within the document. If necessary, modifications to the draft document are made and that revised draft will be forwarded to all of the planning-lab participants one week prior to the plan review meeting for preparation of the review meeting.

Creating a Culture of Learning with Roadmap Review

The facilitator will meet with the planning participants for a consensus review of the draft document. Participants would be encouraged to provide input for changes to the verbiage of the document and the facilitator will execute changes as agreed by the majority of the attendees.

Final Draft Submittal and Presentation

The plan is formally presented to the Board of Education for approval or review (dependent upon the structure of the local organization) by selected Planning Participants assisted by the facilitator.

DETAILS OF THE PLANNING PROCESS

As stated earlier in the book, it is vital to understand the best practices in that they form the basis for the first activity of the process, "Where Are You Now?"—the assessment. We spent seven chapters outlining best practices for each silo and will first outline how those best practices drive the assessment.

The function of the assessment has two primary goals. The first is to assess the district against the best practices. This is a very high-level assessment, looking only at the general trends but it requires a person or group of people with expertise in the three areas described in chapter 2. You may remember at one point we discussed that the seven silos can be divided down into three primary areas: People, Places, Things. Those are the areas of expertise you need for the assessment.

It would be unusual to find one person with expertise in how schools operate who also has expertise regarding school facilities and their infrastructure, the instructional technology systems, and technical systems and components. For the district executing this process itself, you should expect that you will need to form a team of people from within the organization reflecting those four areas of expertise.

It is suggested they use three levels of ratings for the assessment: (1) The district does not have the best practice or part of a best practice, or something similar, in place; (2) The district has the best practice in place but is in the process of creating a culture where the best practice is utilized by the majority of the organizational members; (3) The district has the best practice in place and has a mature culture where the practice is utilized by the majority of the organization.

The second goal of the assessment is to enable the people who will be facilitating the planning process to become familiar with the district culture. It is important for the facilitator(s) to have a firm grasp of the strengths and weaknesses of that particular district's culture. It will be helpful during the planning process in directing the facilitator(s) regarding which issues are important and how to guide the participant discussions.

Checklists

The first step of the assessment is to generate a list of questions to use as a set of reminders during the various interviews and site walkthroughs. There is simply too much information to attempt the assessment without a checklist of the things you need to check. You will need to generate lists related to those three general categories. The technical support and instructional technology questions will be split into two categories. We suggest the following sets of assessment checklists using the questions from the end of chapters 3 through 9 as guides:

PEOPLE
- ☑ Policy, Executive-, Building-, and Classroom-Level Interviews Checklist
- ☑ This checklist contains key questions from:
  - What/How Students Learn
  - Professional Development
  - Policies and Processes
- ☑ Technical Support—People issues

PLACES
- ☑ Walkthrough Checklist
  - Facilities

- Infrastructure
- Systems and Loose Equipment—Existing

THINGS
- ☑ Technology
  - Technical Support—ITIL issues
  - Systems and Loose Equipment

It would be helpful to provide a little more definition of the terms used for the interview groups. Within the context of facilitating development of a five-year roadmap, the policy level is essentially the superintendents' cabinet or direct reports and it may also include the Board of Education. Executive level is the department heads and their direct reports. Building level people are your principals, and classroom level is the teachers.

The checklists are actually grouped into three separate checklists based on the two major groups interviewed and facility visits. The first is the people interviews, with the technical support separated as noted above.

People Checklist

It is very important to interview the policy-, executive-level, building-level and classroom-level people separate from each other. Part of what we are attempting to assess is whether there is clear and succinct communication regarding expectations coming from the policy/executive level all the way down to the classroom. At the same time, is there a bidirectional ability to communicate from the classroom back up to the executive level?

It is also valuable to interview the departmental leaders separate from the executive level; it seems helpful to interview the departments in their environment. That would include curriculum and instruction, which should include professional development (instructional technology may be part of this group), facilities with maintenance and operations, business office, human resources, and the IT department (now considered technical support).

Human resources? In a number of states, the human resource department has the responsibility to train executive-level staff and principals on the new state teacher and principal evaluation systems. The facilitator(s) may also want to find out if there are technology literacy issues attached to job descriptions and new postings.

The facilitator(s) should ask the exact same set of questions from "What/How Students Learn" and the "Professional Development" silos for all four sets of the separate interviews of policy-, executive-, building-, and classroom-level personnel. Documenting those answers and comparing them to each other will provide an excellent overview of how the district views itself. It also gives a clear indication of how consistent the vision for learning and the policies that support that vision is across all levels of operations in the district.

The classroom-level interviews do not touch on the questions from the "Policies and Processes" silo but you do want to obtain responses from the policy-, executive-, and building-level personnel separately for those questions. There should be similar answers from all levels. Otherwise, there is a major roadblock affecting the efficiency and sustainability of the district's learning and teaching culture.

Places Checklist

Of the three checklists, this is the simplest in that there are no interviews of personnel. It is purely a matter of walking around various campuses and observing what you see as prompted by the questions from the "Places and Infrastructure" silos. When this assessment process is applied to a larger school district, it is not necessary to visit all campuses. The facilitator(s) need to obtain a high-level view of what is out there. The facilities department should be able to group the facilities by year of construction and perhaps type of construction, reducing the number of buildings requiring a visit to a reasonable number. Once you see one school of a specific age range, you will most likely have seen an example of all facilities in that same age range.

The checklist is primarily comprised of questions from the "Infrastructure and Facilities" silos. However, you will also want to pay attention to how classrooms are constructed as it relates to the installation of projectors and sound-field enhancement systems. Where would you install the projector? Where is AC power available? What will you use as the projection surface and how does that relate to existing marker boards?

The existing technical support spaces, TR and TCs, should be assessed with regard to compliance with the ANSI/TIA/EIA room size/configuration and cable-installation standards. While in the closets you would want to confirm the manufacturer and model of switches and category of data cable. The switches and category level of the cable should match the information you gain through the IT department interview and questions related to the data network.

Things Checklist

The third checklist has four distinct parts focusing on technical support, using a few organizational questions from the "Policies and Processes" silo and all of the questions from the "Technical Support" and "Systems and Loose Equipment" silos. Again, scheduling a meeting with this group as a separate entity and requesting key support people within the department to attend yields the best results. The one set of variables on the second checklist and this interview is the instructional technology AV system (including clocks, intercom, and sound systems) and IP security cameras. If the district has not relocated responsibility for those systems into the technology department, then a second set of interviews with the department(s) responsible for those systems will be required.

Typically, the organizational structure questions under the "Policies and Processes" silo start the process, confirming connections to and communications with, or lack thereof, curriculum and instruction. It will also contain a list of all technology systems in the district requiring identification of whom within the district has responsibility for maintenance and upkeep. That information should also indicate how service requests for all of those systems are handled.

The second part of the technical support checklist deals with the quantity and type of personnel, both learning and teaching support and technology systems support. If the learning and teaching support personnel (see the definition in chapter 6) are not part of the technical support group, a separate interview with the pertinent department is required. It is important to obtain a reasonable picture of how many people are tasked with what responsibilities. Part of the assessment is to determine whether they have a sufficient number of support personnel and what needs to happen as they add student computing devices.

The third part of the technical support checklist revolves completely around the ITIL management process for IT as outlined in chapter 6. It cannot be overemphasized how important it is for your IT services to follow one of the IT management structures. As the diagrams in chapter 6 indicate, there are twelve primary processes with almost thirty subprocesses involved in the ITIL management framework. One of the harder aspects of this part of the assessment is to determine if the IT department is using processes that accomplish the same thing as ITIL but do not follow the specific methodology of ITIL.

The fourth part of the technical support checklist starts with the questions related to the automated process listed at the end of chapter 6 and then addresses all of the questions associated with chapter 9: Systems and Loose Equipment. The facilitator(s) should start with the interview with IT to obtain answers to a number of those questions but, as mentioned previously, they should have a number of them in mind when visiting campuses as to verify what is heard and seen as being similar.

Data Acquisition

During the assessment process, there is quite a bit of data the facilitator(s) will need to start gathering. Some of the data assists in gaining a picture of the district and the remainder will be used when generating the actual learning and teaching roadmap document. There are four categories of data to request: Learning and Teaching Information, Budgetary Expenditures, Technology Inventory, and Facility Floor Plans (room inventory). Within each category data should be requested relating to:

Learning and Teaching Information

- Any district-based twenty-first-century initiatives or documents
- Any district professional-development plans, structures, or initiatives regarding twenty-first-century learning
- Any state Department of Education twenty-first-century teaching and learning documents
- Any state Department of Education teacher and principal evaluation systems
- Curriculum and instruction structure, positions, and quantity of personnel

The majority of information in this category enables the facilitator(s) to gain an overview of the district, which means it should be reviewed prior to the first planning lab. It also assists in ensuring the facilitator(s) does not commit the cardinal sin of disconnecting this planning process from prior initiatives or invalidating a prior initiative, which is political suicide. Even if the initiative is not accomplishing its own goals, the amount of work exerted by a specific group of people, most likely also involved in this planning process, makes it vital to find an avenue to validate and build this work on prior initiatives.

A primary goal of this planning process is to take ALL of the initiatives, plans, and discussion regarding twenty-first-century learning and pull them into a coherent plan. This planning process will be crippled if it does not take into account prior district activities.

The last item on the list, information regarding curriculum and instruction structure and quantity of personnel, relates directly to learning and teaching coaches. As noted in chapters 5 and 6, job-embedded professional development delivered by qualified and trained learning and teaching coaches is critical to changing the learning culture of a school district. We also reviewed how the interdisciplinary approach to content of the CCS implies a realignment of various curriculum support and instructional support positions. It is valuable to have executive-level discussions prior to the second planning lab regarding how the district may want to approach realigning positions toward learning and teaching coaches.

Budgetary Expenditures for three school years (including this year and two prior)

- Operating budget expenditure for technology support (systems and instructional)
- Operating budget expenditure for software or software licenses
- Operating budget expenditure for computer refresh (replacing existing computers)
- Operating budget expenditure for network maintenance and upgrade
- Operating budget expenditure for AV components and systems (projectors, interactive whiteboards, sound-field enhancement systems)
- Grant expenditures, including E-Rate, for technology (differentiate sources and types of technology)
- Capital expenditures for computer refresh (replacing existing computers)
- Capital expenditures for AV components and systems (projectors, interactive whiteboards, sound-field enhancement systems)

Construction Program Estimates

- Allocations from the construction and fixtures, furnishings, and equipment (FF&E) for technology
- Any local funding for computing devices

The planning process needs to account for its impact on both operating and capital budgets. Even districts that do not have any major construction projects will need to understand how to realign their computer and AV refresh funds. Given the more restrictive economic conditions of today's climate, using three years of historical data should realistically enable projections for the next five years. Every state has different mechanisms for how they manage school budgets; it may be appropriate to dig to find the correct allocation categories. If the planning process includes a construction program, the facilitator(s) will need to acquire the program cost allocations for technology, computing devices, and software associated with the construction program.

Technology Inventory:

- Technology initiatives or policies related to twenty-first-century learning and BYOD
- Technology department (including instructional technology) structure, positions, and quantity of personnel

- Number of data ports wired with minimum CAT 5e cable
- Number and type of data switches
- Number and type of wireless access points
- WAN or MAN configuration and Internet point of presence (POP)
- Number and age of large-screen projectors (differentiate mounted or mobile)
- Number, size, and manufacturer of interactive whiteboards
- Number of sound-field enhancement systems
- Number and age of teacher workstations and laptops
- Number and age of administrative workstations
- Number and age of student workstations and laptops

As noted in chapter 9, moving a school district forward to a digital learning or even digital content instructional culture will require realigning of the technology resources of the district. This realignment cannot be accomplished overnight and we need to know where the Learning and Teaching roadmap is starting from. If the Learning and Teaching roadmap includes upgrades, this information is vital.

If the district has a construction program or technology upgrade initiative:

Facilities:
- Floor plans with indication of types of spaces (type of space inventory)

Part of answering the final question of "How Will You Get There?" requires determining whether the technology fund allocations of a construction program or technology upgrade initiative are sufficient to meet the technology needs. The simplest method I have found is to use a very high-level inventory of types of spaces. The categories used for spaces will be defined when we work through what are called technology frameworks. They are developed on the second day of the first planning lab. If existing floor plans do not indicate the type of space, the fire escape plan from the local campus will give you a clear indication of the types of spaces in the facility.

The interview process and site walkthroughs should occur no more than thirty days prior to the first planning lab. Obviously, the size of the district will dictate how long it will take to complete the high-level assessment.

The assessment must also include the new or replacement spaces contained within the construction program. Most districts should be apply to provide the architectural "program requirements" used to generate a cost estimate for the construction program. That program estimate will have an inventory of spaces contained with the estimate. That construction program space inventory needs to be reconciled with the existing space inventory regarding which existing spaces will be replaced by new construction.

Once the assessment is complete and prior to the first planning lab, it is always beneficial to have a debrief meeting with the executive/cabinet level of the organization to discuss the findings.

There is one critical task to complete between the time of the assessment and the first planning lab. Ensure that the school establishes a "Domain" within one of the cloud-based office suite applications. The planning process will require use of collaborative documents by the planning-lab participants throughout the planning process. The district must have that set up with the planning participants granted permission or an account created for them.

PLANNING LAB 1

The first two-day planning lab is where we start to answer the "Where Do You Want to Go?" question. Expect to have twenty-five to sixty people representing all areas of the organization, but more heavily representing the instructional side of the organization. That would be curriculum and instruction, principals, and teachers participating in that lab. There are a number of tasks to be accomplished and a specific order for those activities.

A central feature of this strategic planning process is to defuse or bypass those issues where you will not be able to reach consensus. Within the context of this process, it will typically be an issue that lies outside of the boundaries of this scope of work. Specifically, those issues will fall into one of two categories. (1) It is an issue that does not belong in one of the seven silos. A thorough understanding of the assessment map will help you with those issues. (2) It is an issue representing a decision at a level beyond this group of participants. That would be Board of Education, cabinet, or collective-bargaining agreement.

ESTABLISHING A BASELINE

There are quite a few concepts and terms the participants may not be familiar with, so creating a common language is the first step. A presentation containing the concepts and terms from chapter 1 is a very good place to start. We immediately then move to a presentation regarding the multiple silo model and the Learning and Teaching Roadmap development process outlined in chapter 2. Yes, presentation. After all of the preaching about using twenty-first-century learning methodologies, it starts off by using one of the lower efficiency methods for transferring information.

But you should bring an aspect of *formative assessments* into the process. You can use an app called Poll Everywhere, an audience-response system that works from within a PowerPoint presentation. The participants can respond to questions about the presentation using phones, Twitter, or web browser. The goal is to make sure that everyone understands key concepts. Dependent upon the poll response, you may want to revisit or expand on those key concepts. Feedback from planning participants indicates that handing out copies of the seven-silo diagram and the assessment map from chapter 2 is of value.

The next step is to spend a bit of time creating discussions of how participants need to define student-centered learning in their organization based on external factors. This is a good point to bring in your state standards, the state Department of Education new teacher- and principal-evaluation systems, and their state requirements for online assessments. This is not a presentation but highlights from the actual state documents used to create discussion among the participants based on those highlights.

It may be of value to educate the participants as to how the Federal Title 1 funding mechanism and the NCLB waiver system together have been the driving force of major changes. This is an important activity at the beginning of the planning process in that it moves the discussion from being a "local" issue to a national issue which everyone in the United States is trying to address.

This is not some type of new "thing" that the local school-district cabinet level came up with and wants its teachers to adopt. This is the local school-district cabinet engaging the entire organization in developing a roadmap designed to help everyone meet their new state standards. If your school district has a collective-bargaining agreement with your local teacher association, this is not a local contract issue. It is about a federal and state mandate requiring local organization compliance.

One of the best tools for helping teachers understand how the new CCS requires student-centered learning is to select a section of their state CCS with embedded technology. Then analyze that section from a twenty-first-century-learning methodology, student technology-literacy and teacher technology-literacy viewpoint. A detailed example is located in chapter 4 under the section about teacher technology literacy. If you choose the correct section, that analysis will clearly depict just how different the CCS really is and how the new state teacher-evaluation systems reflect those differences. It should eliminate any discussion regarding whether teachers need to change their approach to their daily instructional activities.

Starting with the morning activities, the facilitator(s) should have two large flip charts with removable sheets that have adhesive on the top back side of the sheet available in the room. Throughout the two-day session, they are listening to the participant dialogue for what we call a "hindrance" or "obstacle" to the implementation of a student-centered twenty-first-century learning and teaching culture in the district.

An obstacle is an issue that has the potential to stop the implementation of the roadmap dead in its tracks. If the obstacle is not moved or a "workaround" not created, we are all wasting our time trying to create this strategic planning roadmap. A hindrance is something that has an effect on the efficiency of the roadmap implementation.

As the facilitator(s) hears a key concept expressed as a concern of the planning participants, they write down a word or short phrase that indicates the obstacle or hindrance. They should try to list only two issues per sheet and then place the sheet on an open wall. The concepts will be developed further and used at the end of the second day of the first planning lab.

Starting Up Participant Dialogue

It will take a bit of time before the majority of the planning participants feel comfortable about speaking up. There may be members of the Board of Education participating in an "unofficial" status; the executive level is participating and typical classroom teachers. From the facilitator side, an activity that forces dialogue between the participants should occur immediately after the "Common Language" presentation.

To start the dialogue, use what is called an "Effective Learning and Teaching Gauge" using statements associated with the major categories of issues listed in the "What/How Students Learn" and "Professional Development" silos as delineated on the assessment map. The participants are required to assign a rating number that represents the percentage of students or teachers for which the statement is true, in their opinion. An example for each silo and the rating criteria follows:

- **TWENTY-FIRST-CENTURY EFFECTIVE LEARNING** Students consistently participate in student-centered twenty-first-century learning activities aligned to the state standards with embedded technology integration where appropriate.
- **TEACHERS UTILIZE TWENTY-FIRST-CENTURY LEARNING AND TEACHING** Teachers consistently utilize effective best

practices for student-centered twenty-first-century learning and teaching in their respective instructional environments.

Rating Indicator:

1 = Minimal—The statement is true for less than 10 percent of the identified people

2 = Few—The statement is true for 10 percent to 25 percent of the identified people

3 = Some—The statement is true for 26 percent to 75 percent of the identified people

4 = Many—The statement is true for 76 percent to 90 percent of the identified people

5 = Most—The statement is true for 91 percent or more of the identified people

(A copy of the Effective Learning and Teaching Gauge is in the appendix.)

You may notice that the "3" rating represents a rather wide range. That is based on the organizational strategy concept that if 30 percent of the organization's members adopt change, change will occur. You are attempting to obtain a good view of where the participants think the low end occurs in each category so the high end should reflect the symmetry of the low end. It would be of value to note that the participants will typically be more generous as to how their rate their peers in the planning lab versus the assessments conducted through the interviews.

The facilitator(s) should then use a derivative of the "Nominal Group Technique" for generating consensus.

1. The participants are broken up into small groups consisting of five to eight people.
2. Each individual must complete their individual Effective Learning and Teaching Gauge without discussing the gauge with their peers.
3. Once each individual in a group has completed their gauge, the group must negotiate a method by which they will generate a single gauge number representing their group for each statement. The group is allowed to use any method to arrive at a consensus. (The primary point is to force discussion and collaboration, creating engagement for the individual participants.)

The results from each group are entered into a spreadsheet array that provides a graph of the individual group responses and a separate graph of the average. Looking at the general trends, the facilitator(s) determines where groups are diverging from the norm and ask those groups to explain their thought processes behind how they arrived at their ratings.

It may of value to acknowledge that at this stage of the first planning lab the participants are missing a substantial amount of information. That lack of information may result in some participants misinterpreting some of the statements and their responses may not represent a true response to the statement. I am not making the following statement to be cynical, but "We have realistic data gathered from the assessment phase." While the data gathered may be informative, it is more important to kick-start the engagement process of the planning-lab participants.

Informing Participants of Primary Issues and Best Practices

With the participants now engaged and primed for discussion, they need to work through the concepts and processes related to the best practices of all seven silos. You have read through chapters 3 through 9 and you know there is a substantial amount of information to be shared. However, a simple presentation of the information related to each silo will quickly disengage the planning-lab participants. To date, the best process that informs the participants of what they do not know and keeps them engaged is as follows:

1. Have the participants gather into four groups based on the grade levels they work with; PreK–2, 3–5, 6–8, and 9–12. Executive- and policy-level participants can attach to any of the groups and you want to ensure that the technology-systems-support participants do not cluster into one group.
2. The facilitator then provides diagrams or very simple and short PowerPoint presentations covering the primary concepts within a specific silo. (A suggested list is below.)
3. At the end of each silo overview, the facilitator tasks each group to have a discussion regarding the issues of that silo and specifically how their district compares. They should also identify any issues that they perceive as a hindrance or obstacle to the implementation of the plan which will result from the planning process.
   a. There are two silos that also have "special" tasks:
      i. For the "What/How Students Learn" silo, the groups are to discuss what a student computing device should be capable of providing to the student.
      ii. For the "Professional Development" silo, the groups are to discuss what a teacher computing device should be capable of providing to the teacher.

4. Ensure that at least one person in each group has a netbook, tablet, or laptop and that person also has access to the cloud office suite domain. One person should record a simple statement of the findings derived from the discussion within their group. (Note: if a document is opened from the domain, it is automatically saved as soon as someone provides input.)

5. The facilitator manages a "report out" from each group. That may include clarifications of terms and concepts or questions raised by other groups or even disagreement that a specific best practice would work in their district. This is a critical point for the facilitator to be aware of the hindrances and obstacles that seem common between groups. The facilitator should also be aware that a number of the hindrances and obstacles brought up will be subsets of a larger issue. Always use the primary categories of the assessment map to guide your management of how issues are clustered.

6. You repeat this process for all silos, perhaps with the exception of "Facilities" and "Infrastructure." *With the exception of the Learning Space and Furniture under "Facilities," planning for those silos is typically part of a capital fund program that lies outside the purview of this planning process. Yes, this planning process should inform and drive aspects of "Facilities" and "Infrastructure" but the primary planning for those silos occur with facilities and other external consultants (architects and engineers).*

The selection of which best practice within each silo should or should not be used is partially informed by the assessment process conducted only a few weeks prior. We are bouncing a number of concepts off the participants to see which concepts have stickiness. A summary of best practices typically covered within each silo would include:

What/How Students Learn

- Vision for student-centered Twenty-First-Century Learning and Teaching
- Equity of Access
- Data-Driven Student Learning
- Digital Environment (includes Digital Learning vs. Digital Content)
- Student Technology Literacy

Professional Development

- Multistrand Professional Development
- Scope and Sequence Matrix
- Teacher Technology Literacy

- Accountability
- Teacher and Principal Efficacy (Digital Tools)

Policies and Processes

- Keeper of The Plan
- Organizational Structure
- Communication Channels and Roles
- Hardware and Software Adoption Process
- Quality Management
- Funding

Technical Support

- Organizational Structure
- Learning and Teaching Coaches
- Systems Support
- Service Desk
- ITIL Standards
- Disaster Recovery

Facilities

- Furniture
- If this plan is associated with a construction project:
  - Flexible Learning Spaces
  - Extended Learning Spaces (large and small)
  - Learning Families and Communities

Saystems and Components

- Dirty Little Secret About Technology in Schools
- Implications of Internet Access (WAN)
- Wireless Networking
- Communications (VoIP and Paging Systems)
- Instructional Technology
  - Concepts of Viewable Image Requirements
  - Interactive Boards
  - Projectors
  - Sound-Field Enhancement Systems or Audio Playback
  - Integrated AV Systems
  - Document Cameras
  - Concept of a Presentation Station

After completion of the "Overview of the Systems and Components" silo, the facilitator needs to confirm that the participants understand the differences between digital learning and digital content using the audience-response system.

Once you are assured that the concept is established, you move to creating what is called a "Technology Framework." It is the participants' view of what an *ideal* instructional space would look like within the district. The technology framework is an illustration (drawing) of what a typical instructional space in the district should be capable of providing regarding technology and access. The following diagram is an example of what a minimum "Typical Classroom—Technology Framework" would look like for a district implementing digital learning for their elementary- and middle-school instructional spaces. Some of the key aspects of this technology framework are:

- Six student computing devices per classroom
- One teacher computing device
- Wireless network access point (high-density wireless network)
- Two HDMI monitors with keyboard and mouse for small-group work using student device
- LED interactive projector
- Wall or marker board with projection/marker material as projection surface
- Sound-field enhancement system
- Desktop as main presentation station
  - HDMI to projector and desktop LCD display
  - Wireless keyboard
  - Desktop connects to building network via Wi-Fi (enables next item)
  - Connects to student and teacher computing devices via Wi-Fi using app on computing devices
- One VoIP handset

NOTE 1: Every four rooms would share one cart with sufficient student devices that when added to the six in the instructional space, enables every student in that room to have a device.

NOTE 2: Every three high-school instructional spaces would share two carts with fifteen student computing devices in each cart.

If the school district has a construction program occurring during the period of time covered by the Creating a Culture of Learning Plan with Roadmap, the facilitator(s) would work through all of the other types of spaces involved in the construction program, creating technology frame-

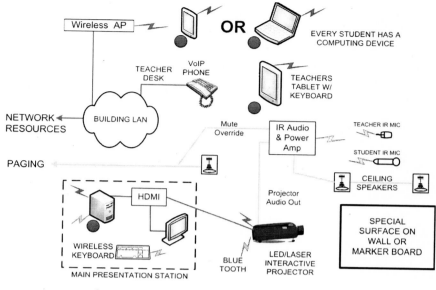

Student and Teacher Devices Connected to Main Presentation Computing Device Using WiFi Network and Up To Projector

works and detailing how they would vary from the typical classroom. That list would include but not be limited to:

Extended Learning Areas—As noted in chapter 7, extended learning areas enable collaborative learning between small groups and large groups. How should technology support those spaces?

Self-Contained Classrooms—Are there dedicated rooms for the more "challenged" students? How are those rooms different? Remember, student computing devices are desktops, not web-browser computing devices.

Science Labs—How are students grouped when working on projects? Students need science probes and simple data loggers that connect to student computing devices. Should the teacher demonstration table be permanent or mobile or some other alternative (using one student station)?

Foreign-Language Labs—There are cloud-based applications available, which means each student needs a computing device with USB headset and microphone.

Content-Specific Computer Labs—There are specific content areas, typically at high-school grade level, requiring every student to have access to a desktop computer running a specific program on that computing unit; for example, architecture/engineering modeling and simulations, graphics, digital photography, accounting, AV production. (Otherwise, there is no need for a computer lab.)

Fine Arts Suite—An elementary-school music teacher pointed out that virtually all state curriculums have aspects of student learning to self-evaluate and self-critique their performances. Since all performances essentially occur in the actual instructional space, those spaces should have real-time AV recording and playback capability. That function requires a special AV system with reasonable quality audio playback.

Media Center—The media center migrates to a more project-based environment when every classroom has computing devices for student research and exploration. Dependent on grade level and size of student population, there will be one or instructional spaces located in the media center.

Digital Creation/Production Facility—Most schools have some type of digital creation/production capacity. What should the technology be capable of providing based on the grade level of the facility? Perhaps this function would also be expanded out to the extended learning areas.

Commons and Assembly Areas—Cafeterias, gyms, and all mixed versions of the two, along with auditoriums, will require some type of AV presentation systems. What technology should be available in these spaces to enable instructional or meeting activities?

Conference Rooms—What type of technology should be available for conference rooms dependent on size of meetings that can be held in the space?

Office Areas and Office Suites—An office is a location where a member of the organization requires access to voice and data communications (phone and computing device) in order to execute their responsibilities. A suite is a cluster of offices with a central reception area. What technology should be available in the reception area?

When the Learning and Teaching Roadmap is associated with a construction program, all of the other frameworks are a derivative of that basic instructional space with the exception of fine arts suite and commons and assembly areas, offices, and office suites. Once that first framework and the concepts are worked through, the remainder of the frameworks proceed fairly quickly.

At this point readers can recognize that this planning process, while not being a "Technology Planning" process, has a huge impact on technology. It directly connects the district vision for learning to technology. Your technology acquisitions are driven by the vision for learning, eliminating major purchases that are considered a mistake at a later date.

Defining Hindrances and Obstacles

Across the prior day and a half, the facilitator(s) have been listening to the dialogue and have listed some of the hindrances and obstacles that need to be addressed to assure a successful implementation of the Learning and Teaching Roadmap. It is now time to complete an exercise regarding those hindrances and obstacles.

The goal is for the participants to engage in discussion and articulate, in their language, what is the actual issue behind the key word or phrase written down. The facilitator(s) simply chooses a topic and requests the participants to clarify and define the issue. As the discussion proceeds, there may be the need to create additional issues or combine issues under a common title.

There may even be the need for the facilitator(s) to list an issue, based on his or her understanding of the assessment map, which the participants did not suggest as a hindrance or obstacle. The facilitator(s) needs to keep good notes regarding the consensus articulation of what the issue represents.

A major point for readers is my experience has been that a typical planning process can manage up to approximately fifteen hindrances or obstacles within the allotted time for Planning Lab 2. More issues than fifteen or so can be handled through two different methods. The facilitator needs to keep them in mind, planning for the second lab.

The facilitator(s) can review the issue list and identify specific issues which the facilitator(s) could handle outside of the planning lab. There are five issues that typically fall into this category:

Formal Communication Channels and Roles—It is common for the building- and classroom-level planning-lab participants to consider the communication between departments as a low-level-impact issue. It is simply not a category representing problems to the typical teacher or sometimes principal. Should the facilitator(s) observe that the planning participants rank the issue low, the facilitator(s) should take this issue as an item to be developed outside the planning lab.

IT Department—Educational organization members at all levels lack a detailed understanding of the tasks and activities of their own IT department. They also lack understanding regarding the standards the department should be using as the basis of its operation. It may be appropriate for the facilitator with expertise in IT operations to generate the goals, strategies, and action items addressing the IT department issue.

Capital Budget—This is another area of education organization operations that the typical organization member does not usually experience. It may be appropriate for the facilitator with expertise with facilities to work with the IT/technology facilitator to develop the goals, strategies, and action items associated with the capital budget.

Operating Budget—The operating budget is typically the purview of cabinet-level and Board of Education–level organization members. It may be appropriate for a facilitator(s) to develop the goals, strategies, and action items while maintaining phone and e-mail contact with key members of those levels.

Another method for addressing a high number of issues Planning Lab 2 participants will need to address is to create a larger number of work groups with fewer members in each group. A suggestion: at least five but not more than eight participants in each work group. How hindrance and obstacle workgroups are formed and the tasks they work through are detailed under the Planning Lab 2 activities.

Once the participants feel that all of the hindrances and obstacles specific to their district have been identified, they need to prioritize the issues. There are three categories of prioritization:

High-Level Impact—It is the opinion of the planning-lab participants that this Learning and Teaching Roadmap will be severely limited; perhaps to the point of failure, regarding its impact on establishing a student-centered twenty-first-century learning and teaching culture in the district, if this issue is not addressed and resolved.

Medium-Level Impact—It is the opinion of the planning-lab participants that the efficiency of this Learning and Teaching Roadmap will be substantially reduced, diminishing its impact on establishing a student-centered twenty-first-century learning and teaching culture in the district, if this issue is not addressed and resolved.

Low-Level Impact—It is the opinion of the planning-lab participants that this issue does not represent an item that will cause any concerns about the success of this Learning and Teaching Roadmap, but resolution of this issue will greatly increase the efficiency, reducing the amount of friction that must be overcome when implementing the plan.

We then use what would be called a *cumulative voting* method. If you remember, the facilitator(s) use a "Post-it" type of flip-chart paper and list only two issues per sheet. Those sheets should be adhered to the walls around the meeting location. The facilitator(s) should review one more time what the group has identified as the issue related to each key word or phrase.

They then hand out a set of colored stickers to the participants. The quantity of stickers should be equal to or slightly less than the number of issues listed on the flip-chart sheets and equally divided into three colors, each sticker representing one vote. Try to use red for High-Impact, yellow for Medium-Impact, and green for Low-Impact votes. Each participant can place only one sticker (one vote) on one issue.

Once the participants have completed their votes, it is very easy to see the impact level the participants perceive each issue belongs in. The caution is that all issues cannot be in the High-Impact or Medium-Impact category; the issues need to be prioritized. It may require some discussion, clarification, and persuasion by the facilitator(s) to move issues to lower categories so there is a reasonable distribution of all issues.

The last exercise of the first Planning Lab is to circle back around to the Mission for Twenty-First-Century Learning and Teaching discussion. That discussion should have been the first best practice discussed with the participants after the Learning and Teaching Gauge activity. Based on all of the input and dialogue over the prior two days, the participants are required to articulate the main concepts they think should be contained within their district's mission statement for student-centered twenty-first-century learning and teaching.

Once those key concepts have been identified, the participants are assigned homework to bring back to the next planning lab. The participants are to use the key concepts and create a district mission statement for student-centered twenty-first-century learning and teaching.

They are also supposed to create a teacher rubric reflecting that mission statement, which the staff would use on a daily basis to ensure they are aligning their student experiences with the mission statement. Brain research clearly indicates that most people can only remember and recall three to five things at a time. Therefore, the teacher rubric should have a least three but no more than five steps the teachers use to ensure they are meeting the district's expectations regarding their instructional activities.

The best method for encouraging development of these documents is to post a form with the key concepts on Google Docs and enable the participants to pull up, develop, and post their version or work collaboratively with others. Using Google Docs is great in that everyone can see the various versions.

PREPARATION FOR PLANNING LAB 2

Planning Lab 2 is focused on articulating the steps the participants expect the district to take in order to move from their current learning and teaching culture toward a student-centered twenty-first-century learning

and teaching culture. There are a number of preparations that should occur between the planning labs. While there is no particular order to the
preparations, the tasks can be grouped based on some general categories:

Budgets Preparation

It is very hard to predict the conditions associated with operating and
capital budgets that will be encountered as part of a Learning and Teaching Roadmap. The range of possible scenarios is quite large. Should readers plan to facilitate this planning process on their own, they will need to
be flexible and nimble regarding how the budgeting process is handled.
The following sections provide an overview of the revenue and expense
budgets which impact the planning process.

Based on the information gathered as part of the data-acquisition
process of the assessment, the facilitator(s) needs to generate a projected
operating and capital revenue estimate associated with this plan.

Operating Budget Revenue—With regard to the operating budget
revenue stream, prior to Planning Lab 2, we have no indication of
how the Learning and Teaching Roadmap will impact the operating
budget but we need a starting point of the categories and amounts
in each category. It is very critical to the process that the revenue/
expense projections are based on real funds that the district and
facilitator(s) know, within a reasonable range of flexibility, will be
available. Do not use any fund sources that cannot be confirmed as
available throughout the five-year plan timeline. Utilizing the three-
year historical data gathered during the assessment phase, project an
annual operating budget revenue stream. This planning process en-
compasses five years; therefore, the operating budget revenue should
be projected out for at least five years.

Capital Budget Revenue—The capital budget process, both revenue
and expenses, is more of a straightforward process.

• Capital Budget Revenue (No Construction Program)—If there is no
construction program involved and its associated capital budget for
technology, the primary task will be a reallocation of existing capital
expenditures associated with computing devices and AV components. Using the historical data gathered during the assessment
phase, project a revenue stream for the next five years. Dependent
upon the E-Rate reimbursement rate of the district, there may be
an opportunity to leverage the E-Rate "Internal Connections" funds
toward updates of the wired and wireless networks of the district.
Typically, your reimbursement rate must be in the mid-eighties to

qualify for those funds and the actual cutoff point varies from year to year.

- Capital Budget Revenue (With Construction Program)—If there is a construction program occurring during the timeline of the plan, we need to pull that information into the revenue stream in addition to the historical information mentioned in the prior paragraph. That will require someone with knowledge of how school districts organize budgets for construction. There are at least five categories of fund sources and how they are used will change for every school district regardless of which state they are in. The first four are associated with revenue generated from the sale of bonds that are backed by tax revenue. The fifth are funds provided by the district from other sources:
  - Construction Costs for Technology—These budgets may be in the electrical cost estimate or a stand-alone budget, but there will be a dollar allocation per square foot of new or renovated space construction for those systems that are incorporated into the building construction. That would be the data cabling and cabinets, paging or intercom systems, public address systems for common and assembly areas, AV systems and cabling for classrooms, and clock system. These funds are controlled by the architectural/engineering team.
  - FF&E—All projects have a category of costs for furniture and other loose equipment. It is important to determine if there are any technology allocations within the FF&E budget for loose equipment such as data network hardware (wired and wireless), displays, and so on. In most states, these funds are controlled by the district. I am aware of only one state where these funds are controlled by the architectural/engineering team.
  - Bond-Based District Allocations—In some states, the school districts have the authority to create fund allocations within a bond for projects other than the general construction. These could be deferred maintenance (roofs and HVAC replacement), technology systems, or computing device, servers, and so on. The point is to determine what the state rules are and understand if there are any technology allocations in this category of revenue.
  - Construction Contingencies—When a district is involved in a construction program, the only thing you can be assured of is that things will not work out the way you expect them to. The range of things that can go wrong or right is large. Therefore, all programs will have a category of funds, controlled by the district and typically subject to Board of Education approval, to handle those unknown factors. It is not a small amount of revenue; it will typi-

cally be somewhere between 3 and 5 percent of the of the gross construction budget. We will not be using these funds as part of our revenue stream estimate but it is important to know how much is in these funds. Sometime during the planning process, it would be of value to explore the possibility of the executive committee and Board of Education making a commitment that any project contingency funds would be allocated to providing the new technology in existing facilities.

- Local Capital Funds—Computing devices, the software used by those devices, and the servers that service computing devices are not long-life-cycle products. Bond revenue is typically funds paid back over a twenty-year or more period of time. There are a number of reasons why it may not be appropriate to fund a five-year-life-cycle item with twenty-year money. (Some school districts have absolutely no other choice and will use twenty-year money to purchase five-year-life-cycle items.) Does the district have a special allocation for technology from revenue sources other than the bond program?

Existing Inventory—We will use the existing inventory of computing devices, video displays, and classroom instructional tools gathered during the assessment and calculate a value for that existing inventory. The method of how we estimate that value will be outlined in the upcoming section about capital budget cost estimate.

Technology Frameworks

If the district has a construction program occurring during the timeline of the Learning and Teaching Roadmap, the facilitator(s) need to complete all of the various technology frameworks developed during Planning Lab 1. As noted in the capital budget costs estimate, these graphical representations of technology capability for every space in the district drive the technology program cost estimate.

Estimated Costs

It is important to simplify the planning process and one of the methods used for this planning process is to develop a high-level (ballpark) capital cost estimate associated with the roadmap. The "Inventory of Types of Spaces" gathered during the assessment phase should have utilized the same space categories as the technology frameworks.

It is important to realize that an error of a few spaces in each building will have little impact on the gross budget. This is a first-level estimate and we simply want to determine if the available revenue comes close to matching our capital cost needs. There are a number of methods that could be used to arrive at that estimate but the following is known to work.

A quick overview of the process is to point out that it will first determine the total cost of a technology program, as if the district has nothing in place. It then takes away the existing inventory and the differential represents the capital cost requirements to bring all spaces in the district up to the ideal technology implementation represented by the technology frameworks.

Capital Cost Estimate—Using simplified spreadsheets the facilitator(s) need to:

- Generate a spreadsheet that lists the types of spaces used for the technology in columns and each facility within the district on a row. From the inventory of types of spaces, simply input the quantity of each type of space for that facility and then total each column. We now have a total quantity of each type of space in the district. You could call this a "Quantity of Spaces" spreadsheet.
- Generate a second spreadsheet that lists the types of technology (i.e., data port, teacher device, student device, main presentation station, projector, sound-field enhancement system, data closet, etc.) in columns. The types of spaces are in rows. From the technology frameworks, enter the quantity of each type of technology for that type of space in its respective column. Multiply the quantities of types of technology times the quantity of that type of space and generate sums of the columns. You now have the total quantity of each type of technology required for the entire district to be upgraded to the ideal technology implementation. You may want to call this a "Quantity of Technology by Space" spreadsheet.
- Generate a third spreadsheet that uses the quantity of technology information from the prior worksheet. You create groupings of systems and components, such as data cabling and network hardware (switch and wireless components); computing devices, servers, and storage; VoIP systems and handsets and classroom AV components, and apply a unit cost for each. You extend the unit cost to a total cost for that item and subtotal the costs by the types of systems.
- You copy the third spreadsheet and replace the quantity column with what the district already has in place. You subtract the total of this spreadsheet from the prior spreadsheet and you now have a capital budget cost estimate associated with an ideal technology implementation. Add at least 5 percent as a contingency (items you may have missed). The only other impact to this number would be

costs for furniture coming out of the hindrances and obstacles work taking place in the Planning Lab 2.

When the plan is associated with a construction project or program, you would need to take a different approach to arrive at the total capital budget impact of the plan. I would suggest the following:

- The cost extensions should be divided into three categories of costs. You may want to call this the "Ideal Technology Implementation Cost" spreadsheet.
  - Construction Budget—That technology purchased as part of the construction program allocation for technology (data cabling, closets, paging and sound systems, AV systems for classrooms)
  - FF&E Budget—Those items that are loose equipment items attached to the systems installed under the construction budget (network hardware, phone handsets, flat-panel displays, projectors, video presentation tools)
  * District Purchases—The computing devices associated with the overall technology program (teacher and student computing devices, desktop computer, administration computers, servers, and network software costs)

As mentioned during the revenue source assessment, we should always include contingency funds for unknown factors. Add a 5 percent contingency for each category and total the three categories. We now have a total cost estimate for implementing the ideal technology solution across the entire district.

- Using a blank version of the ideal technology-implementation cost spreadsheet, enter the quantity of existing inventory of technology in the district into the proper row and sum the three categories. We now have an estimate of how much revenue the district has already spent. You may want to call this the "Existing Technology Inventory." When we subtract this total estimate from the prior ideal technology-implementation cost spreadsheet, the differential is a reasonable estimate of how much it will cost in capital budget to bring all spaces in the district to the same level of technology capability (equity).
- Generate a simplified Gantt chart which places the technology implementation activities on a schedule tied to the construction budget (the Roadmap for Technology). The construction program will have a similar document that should be used to drive this chart. The primary purpose of the chart is to inform the planning-lab partici-

pants of when activities funded from the capital budget occur and which specific campuses will have new technology installed. The facilitator(s) should call this the "Capital Activities Timeline."

At this point in the preparation process, the facilitator(s) should have a fairly clear idea whether the revenue available aligns with the estimated costs for the capital budget. (The operational budget impact will be determined by the goals and strategies work for each hindrance and obstacle in Planning Lab 2.) The facilitator(s) will need to have a reconciliation path in mind. That may mean discussion with the district personnel in control of the budget regarding additional fund sources or dialing back the technology implementation to match available funds.

This issue must be addressed and worked out prior to Planning Lab 2. One of the last activities of the lab will be sharing the revenue/cost findings with the participants. You need to have a clear recommendation of what happens when the revenue available does not match your cost estimates.

Hindrances and Obstacles

The facilitator(s) will need to create a Google Docs form for each of the hindrances and obstacles identified during Planning Lab 1. The form should contain:

- Title—The hindrance or obstacle.
- Level of Impact—Indication of the impact level from the prioritization process.
- Group Members—A location where the members of the group who developed the strategies addressing the issue list their names.
- Description—Clearly articulate a description of the issue discussed in Planning Lab 1.
- Goal(s)—The group members should outline the desired outcomes regarding this issue.
- Strategy—Typically, addressing a single issue will require multiple strategies. Provide up to four strategy sections with each containing:
  - *Description of the Strategy*—The group members need to clearly articulate the specifics of the strategy they have in mind.
  - *Activity*—What activities do the group members see as necessary to move the strategy forward?
  - *Responsibility*—Who within the organization should be responsible for ensuring the activities occur?
  - *Timeline*—What is the timeline during which these activities should take place?

- *Costs*—Are there any costs associated with any of the activities? If so, the group members should attempt to estimate what those costs would be.
- *Funding Source*—If there are costs associated with any of the activities, what is the expected fund source paying for those costs?

Prior to Planning Lab 2, the facilitator places all of the hindrances and obstacles documents into groups. The number of groups created is a balance between the number of planning-lab participants and the number of hindrances and obstacles; perhaps trying to balance the issues based on the priority assigned by the planning participants, for example: one high-priority, one medium-priority, and one low-priority issue for each group.

PLANNING LAB 2

The first activity of the second planning lab is to review the planning participants' homework assignment. Using the key concepts articulated at the end of the first lab, the planning participants were to develop a Mission for Twenty-First-Century Learning and Teaching for the district and create a teacher rubric associated with the mission. The participants were asked to use a Google Docs form and if possible work collaboratively with other participants (working on the same document at different times while reviewing and commenting on each other's work). This is a great demonstration of how students can work in a collaborative manner when using cloud-based tools.

Bring up the documents and review them with the group. Ask the participants to comment about what they do and do not like. If the participants prefer a particular phrasing in one document and other parts of another document, cut and paste the desired pieces into a common document. Continue with the process until the group reaches a consensus on a district Mission for Twenty-First-Century Learning and Teaching.

Execute the same type of activity regarding the teacher rubric that informs teachers if they are aligning their daily activities to the mission.

The second activity is to review the other findings from the Planning Lab 1. That may include the Learning and Teaching Gauge results, best practices that seem to reflect activities that would be appropriate for the district to adopt, the typical classroom technology framework, and the components it contains. If the Learning and Teaching Roadmap includes a construction program, all of the other technology frameworks should be reviewed for accuracy.

Creating Goals and Strategies

The next activity is to create small groups by each person simply counting off sequentially up to the number of groups required and repeating until everyone is assigned a group. The participants gather with other participants with the same number. Each group will then open up the group of hindrances and obstacles, which were posted to the district "domain" associated with their group number. The facilitator(s) explains the form and what information the groups are expected to provide as indicated by the different sections of the form. The groups simply start working through their issues, filling out the forms for each issue.

Google Docs is preferred for this portion of the planning lab. That application enables true collaborative work between the planning-lab participants. Each individual member can simultaneously look at and make changes to the document as the group works on the document. Or it can be a few people making most of the changes. The exercise will demonstrate and inform the participants of how collaborative student learning could work while using standard word-processing documents. This should model what students are expected to do in the classroom.

As the groups are discussing their issues and developing goals and strategies, the facilitator(s) should be reviewing the work generated by the groups by walking around, interfacing with the small groups, and using the online access to review the documents they are creating. It is important to ensure that each group is staying within the boundaries of its issue. Some overlap between issues should be expected but we do not want two different groups to come up with radically different solutions to the same issue.

As a group finishes with an issue, the facilitator(s) should find an appropriate point to stop all activity and have that group report out to the larger gathering. The facilitator(s) should also direct a discussion regarding the strategies and activities of that issue. The purpose is to generate consensus that the suggested solution aligns with the general perception of the entire group regarding how to address the identified hindrance or obstacle.

Do not rush or skip the reporting out of the strategies and the creation of dialogue about the activities. This is the part of the planning process where the participants make the roadmap a plan that connects directly to who they are and the issues of their district. This activity should create a sense of ownership for the roadmap, which should be used to promote the completed plan to their peers. Upon conclusion of the review and comments regarding the strategies and activities addressing a specific issue, the process continues until all issues have been addressed.

It would be quite unusual for all identified issues to be addressed in one day. With some prior warning, it is appropriate to suspend the group activities for the day with the intention of resuming where they left off the following morning.

During the evening recess, the facilitator(s) need to review a few of the completed high-level impact issues. Then they need to generate a second Gantt chart that places the strategies associated with hindrances and obstacles into a timeline. This chart should be called the "Operational Activities Timeline." The intent is to provide the planning participants with a model of how each strategy and the individual activities will be placed into a timeline and sequence (roadmap).

The facilitator(s) only need to place the activities of three or four issues into the chart and that should be sufficient to provide the planning participants with a concept of how the roadmap and the sequence of activities will work. We do find it very beneficial to color-code the various stages of the strategies; for example, planning, training the trainers, training the users, implementation, and so on.

The participants will continue to work on developing strategies and action plans that address the prioritized hindrances and obstacles that were not completed the prior day. It is not unusual for this activity to utilize a large portion of day two of Planning Lab 2.

Once all of the hindrances and obstacles issues are addressed, it is time to show the participants the budgets and cost estimates. The facilitator(s) should explain how the revenue estimates was obtained and what it looks like for the operating and capital budgets. If the Learning and Teaching Roadmap includes a construction program, the facilitator(s) should share the findings of the construction budget and technology cost estimate. If the technology costs estimate exceeds the funds allocated for that work in the construction budget, the facilitator(s) should hold a discussion of how to reduce the costs and reconcile the revenue and cost streams.

It is also time to review the Technology Implementation Timeline (Gantt Chart) related to a construction project or program. Subsequent to presenting the timeline, the facilitator(s) should generate a discussion of how the timeline may impact the district's professional-development process.

Upon completion or the point where they must stop activities related to hindrances and obstacles strategies and activities, the facilitator(s) need to share the operating activity timeline Gantt chart with the planning-lab participants. The facilitator(s) should explain the concepts behind the chart and generate discussion of what the chart implies to the district. It would be of value to bring back the capital activities timeline chart and generate discussion of how the two charts reflect the activities in each other. Prior to closing this activity, the facilitator(s) should explain that the facilitator(s) will take all of the issues and their respective activities and place them into the chart, providing a five-year overview of activities and timelines.

Defining Success

The final activity of the second planning lab is to facilitate a discussion among the planning-lab participants regarding the definition of a successful roadmap. What conditions would be considered a success at the end of the five-year internal renew of the strategic plan?

The facilitator(s) should utilize the categories related to percentage of users who meet a specific criterion as defined for the Learning and Teaching Gauge used during Planning Lab 1. The following is a review of the ranges used.

Minimal—The statement will be true for less than 10 percent of the identified people

Few—The statement will be true for 10 percent to 25 percent of the identified people

Some—The statement will be true for 26 percent to 75 percent of the identified people

Many—The statement will be true for 76 percent to 90 percent of the identified people

Most—The statement will be true for 91 percent or more of the identified people

Some examples of how past planning-lab participants have defined success for the Learning and Teaching Roadmap follows:

Most teachers and administrators (91 percent of more) understand and execute the district mission for student-centered twenty-first-century learning and teaching on a daily basis.

Many of the students (76 percent to 90 percent) have the technology available when and where they need it to accomplish their student-centered activities.

Many students (76 percent to 90 percent) consistently experience effective twenty-first-century student-centered learning activities in their respective classrooms.

Many teachers (76 percent to 90 percent) can demonstrate an advanced
level of competency for student-centered twenty-first-century learning and teaching methodologies.

Most teachers (91 percent or more) can demonstrate an intermediate
level of competency regarding technology literacy.

Many of the readers will suggest that some of these categories should
be at the 100 percent level. Two cautions:

1. A realistic timeline for a total implementation of student-centered
   twenty-first-century learning and teaching across all grade-level and
   content areas will take seven to eight years for most school districts.
   The concepts behind the Learning and Teaching Roadmap represent
   major cultural shifts within every educational organization. It simply takes time.
2. Every school district will have new students and teachers coming
   into this new environment. How much time will it take for those
   students and teachers to catch up to their peers?

It may be of value to step back and take a larger view of the complex
situation. Research data conclusively indicates that student attitudes and
expectations regarding education are firmly seated by the end of the third
grade. While the change in school district culture regarding learning and
teaching represented by this planning process should engage more students, there will be students who are too far behind to really catch up to
their peers.

That is not to suggest you abandon or not focus on helping those students. It is to simply state that the harsh reality is that students need to be
at the appropriate level of academic achievement for their grade starting
in the second grade to maximize their potential for reaching the college-
or career-readiness goals of the new standards. It will take ten years for
second-graders who experience this new student-centered culture to become high-school seniors. It will simply take quite a bit of time to see the
impact of these changes for all students.

Chapter 11

Creating the Roadmap

This chapter is intended to assist those readers who have attempted to develop a Creating a Culture of Learning Plan with Roadmap with the assembly of the information gathered into a usable document. We will first explore an overview of the document and then provide detailed information about how to generate the various sections.

The typical Learning and Teaching Roadmap has six sections:

- An executive summary
- An introduction with overview of the seven-silo approach focused on "What/How Students Learn"
- "Where Are You Now" section
- "Where Do you Want to Go" section
- "How Will You Get There" section
- Appendix

Once a draft of the document is generated there are two review steps. The first review is by the executive cabinet and Board of Education–level members. After revisions based on executive cabinet and Board of Education comments, a second review occurs, which is best executed as a single-day workshop with as many of the planning-lab participants as possible. The final version of the plan, including an executive summary, is generated based on the planning-lab-participant comments.

Prior to outlining the various sections, it would be beneficial to discuss the timeline for generating various sections. A typical Learning and Teaching Roadmap document is rather large due to the comprehensive scope of the process. When including a construction program, the document can easily climb close to one hundred pages. Without a construction program, it will be closer to eighty pages. The point is that you should not wait until completion of the last planning lab to start writing. It would be very hard to generate such a large document in less than a few weeks after the second planning lab to meet the deadlines for executive cabinet and Board of Education review and comments.

Readers may have noticed the recommendation that the assessment interview and site walkthroughs occur up to thirty days prior to the first planning lab. It would be beneficial to generate the majority of the "Where Are You Now" section after the interviews and site walkthroughs and prior to the first planning lab. If the facilitator(s) have correctly accomplished the tasks from the prior chapter—the interviews, site walkthroughs, and planning labs—the document will essentially write itself. The facilitator(s) need to organize the data but the majority of the work is accomplished through the assessment and planning activities.

In addition to the preparation activities for the second planning lab, try to generate most of the "Where Do You Want to Go" section between the two planning labs. At that point, it leaves a reasonable amount of work to complete subsequent to the second planning lab and prior to a deadline for delivery of the first draft.

INTRODUCTION

The introduction seems to be the best place to provide an explanation to readers of the factors that caused the district to pursue development of the Learning and Teaching Roadmap. It should take only a paragraph or two to provide that information.

The second part of the introduction is used to introduce the reader to the district Mission for Student-Centered Twenty-First-Century Learning and Teaching. Even though the Mission for Student-Centered Twenty-First-Century Learning and Teaching belongs in the "How Will You Get There" section, also placing it in the introduction provides an excellent opportunity to set the tone and focus of the document.

It is also of value to provide an overview of the seven-silo concept and the planning process used to gather the information used in the document. Start the overview with an explanation of when the assessment and planning labs occurred and reference a planning participant list, located in the appendix. Then outline the overall seven-silo philosophy and explain how those seven silos are translated into the assessment map. Then provide an overview of the general sequence to the process and reference the planning participant list located in the appendix.

"WHERE ARE YOU NOW" SECTION

The first main section, which contains information pertinent to the Learning and Teaching Roadmap, is where the facilitator(s) outline their findings from the various interviews and site walkthroughs. Essentially, it is an assessment report. Using the notes from the silo checklists they created, the facilitator(s) should work through the seven silos. Planning-lab-participant feedback regarding the document has led us to use as many graphic indicators as possible, indicating to readers where they are in the document. For the larger sections we use the graphic as above; for the individual silos, we use the graphics readers have observed at the beginning of chapters 3 through 9.

The order of the assessment report follows the same order of the silo descriptions in chapters 3 through 9:

- What/How Students Learn
- Professional Development
- District Policies and Processes
- Technical Support
- Facilities
- Infrastructure
- Systems and Loose Equipment

Readers may remember that the facilitator(s) are using three categories during the assessment. (1) The district does not demonstrate an operational practice similar to the best practice used as the model. (2) The district has an operational practice similar to the best practice used as the model but it is not mature and does not permeate all departments, grade levels, or classrooms. (3) The district has a mature operational practice similar to the best practice used in the model permeating all departments, grade levels, and classrooms.

The facilitator(s) need to use concise and simple statements when reporting about the findings associated with a specific issue. The document is comprehensive in scope and large enough; this section needs to be treated as a fact-finding report. Subsection titles based on the sections contained in each silo chapter with bullet points using summaries of the findings work well. Readers may have noted a number of the interview questions at the end of chapters 3 through 9 are sequential.

If the responses to the first question in the sequence indicate they do not have an operational practice similar to the best practice model, the subsequent questions will be even further off track. The writer only needs to address the first issue in the sequence.

We would also like to point out that the report needs to be an accurate and honest assessment of the district. As members of the organization start to review the document, it is vital to the credibility of the facilitator(s) that the assessment section reflects what the members know is true about their organization. When a report attempts to gloss over or minimize the impact of less-than-positive findings, the report quickly loses credibility.

When the facilitator(s) generate this portion of the document prior to the first planning lab, it informs them with a much clearer understanding of the district issues which need to be addressed by the Learning and Teaching Roadmap. They are better prepared to facilitate the planning labs.

It seems of value to create a concise and brief summary of the assessment findings at the end of this section of the document.

"WHERE DO YOU WANT TO GO" SECTION

During the planning labs the facilitator(s) were observing which best practices seem to resonate with the planning-lab participants. This second major section should provide succinct descriptions of those best practices which seem to apply to the district.

Similar to the first section, we suggest that the order of best practices should follow the same order of the silo descriptions in chapters 3 through 9. Use the graphics located at the beginning of chapters 3 through 9 for an indication of where the reader is located in the document.

- What/How Students Learn
- Professional Development
- District Policies and Processes
- Technical Support
- Facilities

- Infrastructure
- Systems and Loose Equipment

All Learning and Teaching Roadmaps would have these categories but a roadmap associated with a building program would expand one subsection. The "Systems and Loose Equipment" section would be expanded to include the technology frameworks developed on the second day of the first planning lab. We will use both graphical representations and verbiage describing the systems and loose equipment for the various spaces located in the building program scope of work. We do make it clear that the technology frameworks are the *ideal* implementation the planning-lab participants thought the spaces should be capable of providing, not necessarily what the program budget will enable.

We would suggest the following format of the information:

- Starting with the technology framework for a typical classroom
  - We use the graphical representation, working from the top to the bottom, and generate verbiage describing each type of system, system port, or loose equipment indicated on the drawing similar to the framework provided in chapter 10.
  - At the end of the verbiage description, we insert the actual graphic for the respective framework.
- Once the categories of systems and loose equipment have been described, we do not need to repeat the description.
  - Therefore, subsequent technology frameworks simply provide a list of components and system ports with a quantity of those ports or devices listed in front of the category. (When new components come into play, such as flat-panel displays for conference rooms, we provide verbiage describing the component or system port the first time the new system port of component appears.)
  - After the list of system ports or components and their respective quantities for that specific type of space, we insert the graphics for that specific technology framework.
- The process continues until all technology frameworks have been described.

HOW WILL YOU GET THERE SECTION

The third primary section of the document is the roadmap, which provides a path for the district to move their culture forward to efficient, effective, and sustainable student-centered twenty-first-century learning and teaching. This is the most important section of the planning document.

Start the section off with the Mission for Twenty-First-Century Learning and Teaching. To revisit, this is the primary mission for learning within the district. All members of the organization, from the cabinet level to the classroom level, use this philosophy to drive all aspects of student learning in the district. Everyone thinks about and talks about learning in the same way and understands the expectations of the district regarding classroom activities. It also provides teachers with a clearly articulated and simple set of rubrics they use on a daily basis to inform them whether they are meeting the organization's expectations in their classrooms. If it takes more than a few paragraphs to document this mission, it needs to be reworked and simplified.

The second subsection of this section is a simple reporting out of the goals and strategies developed by the planning-lab participants related to the hindrances and obstacles identified and developed during the planning labs. Each hindrance or obstacle should have a simple color-coded graphic at the beginning of its subsection indicating the impact level of the issue. Past roadmaps have used red to indicate high-level impact, yellow (or gold) to indicate medium-level impact, and green to indicate low-level impact. This section has been written for the facilitators by the planning-lab participants with the exception of any issues the facilitator(s) agreed to address on behalf of the lab participants.

The third subsection relates to the operational budget. It will typically provide an overview of the operational budget revenue as it applies to the roadmap with descriptions of revenue categories. If there are suggested revisions to the operational budget related to this roadmap, then generate a projected five-year operating budget with the proposed changes. The final piece of this section is the operational activities timeline which the facilitator(s) started and presented to the planning-lab participants on the last afternoon of the second planning lab. This is the Gantt chart with all strategies for all hindrances and obstacles placed into their respective timeline, creating a very detailed roadmap of the steps involved to address all of the hindrances and obstacles. It should be accompanied by an explanation of the purpose of the chart and what it actually represents.

The fourth subsection relates to the capital budget. Obviously, if the roadmap includes a building program, this subsection will use the documentation generated for the capital program and capital activities timeline used in the second planning lab. This subsection is similar to the operational budget section and it should stay at a high level without much detail. A number of the roadmaps have the details that support the high-level summary for those readers who are interested. There are a number of roadmaps where executive-level members only wanted the revenue and costs associated with the building program to be explored. They did not want to know what it would cost to upgrade the existing facilities to technology frameworks. It may be different for every school district.

The conclusion of this section is a single page that outlines the definitions of success for this roadmap. This is the work completed by the planning-lab participants on the last afternoon of the second planning lab. It should be a simple, single page of bulleted points outlining the expectations for five years out, at the end of the roadmap timeline.

APPENDIX

Typically the appendix will have a list of the planning-lab participants, perhaps an overview of the planning process, and a list of acronyms used throughout the document. When the planning process includes a large construction project, the cost estimate and revenue reconciliation spreadsheets are posted in the appendix, not in the main body. A summation of those spreadsheets should be used in the main body of the document.

EXECUTIVE SUMMARY

The executive summary does not get generated until completion of all review and comment activities. However, it is a very important section of the document. As noted in prior sections, this Learning and Teaching Roadmap is an internal document. It is not intended for posting on the school district website for general public dissemination. There may be information in the document that you do not want out in public. However, a sanitized executive summary is an excellent document to place on the school district website for public dissemination. This may be the hardest part of the document to generate. How do you compress an eighty- to hundred-page document down to a two- or three-page summary? You work it and rework until it is a clean but succinct summation of the roadmap.

The comprehensive nature of this planning process requires quite a bit of documentation and explanation. The smallest document resulting from this planning process exceeded eighty pages and the more typical document totals around one hundred pages. They are large documents.

It is virtually impossible to use verbiage to explain how to generate a complex document like a Learning and Teaching Roadmap. Obviously, the best way to explain what the document is like is to show you. Therefore, you can find two samples of a Creating a Culture of Learning Plan with Roadmap document at www.meeksgeeks.com. One example includes a large construction program and the other has no construction involved at any point of the plan.

Conclusion

The concept of "aligning the organization" to a common mission statement for student-centered twenty-first-century learning and teaching comes directly from the work of statistician W. Edwards Deming, acknowledged as the father of TQM.

However, current organizational management researchers and theorists have correctly pointed out that using the management methods of the original TQM concepts, which work well for manufacturing, do not work for knowledge-based companies (think Google). Manufacturing TQM combines a consistent churning of statistically sampling products at all stages of the manufacturing process with review, analysis, and proactive suggestions for improvement from a team of people from all of the silos involved in the product: designers, engineers, process engineers, management, and manufacturing line workers.

Their goal is to manufacture a superior product. The average person will typically choose a superior product, meaning the company sells its products, enabling the company to make a profit. Today's service and knowledge-based companies do not have a manufacturing process to monitor and analyze. They end up monitoring their profitability as the health indicator of their organization. Unfortunately that does not work well. By the time the management system indicates there is a problem, too many substandard activities have occurred. It is too late for the organization to fix those substandard activities and they lose profits. Their analysis systems do not provide data in a timely manner.

TQM management for service- or knowledge-based organizations requires something different. Twenty-first-century management methodologies suggest the solution is to measure the activities that make a difference to the clients of the organization. For educators, it will be the student.

Let's paint the issue from an educational viewpoint. Consider a student in your elementary school who has attended from PreK to third grade. Toward the end of the third grade, this student participates in the state-required student assessment tests and fails to meet third-grade academic proficiency expectations. The teachers, the parents, and the principal are surprised!? Wait a minute, that student has been in your system for four years and you had no indicators that this student missed learning things in first grade, which impacted the first assessment in the third grade? How does that student ever catch up?

Does this sound even remotely familiar? If a school district is waiting for the annual student-achievement scores to determine if it has been successful in managing the learning of its students, it will be too late. By the time the results arrive in the district, there is nothing the teachers or principals can do about those outcomes. Their learners missed knowledge that they should have learned months or years ago. There has to be a more real-time connection between data and activities that are planned as a reaction to that data. In schools we call them formative assessments.

The need for formative assessments does not stop with students. Timely data—formative assessments—for teachers and principals indicating alignment to the organization vision for learning in their classrooms and schools is a necessity. That data should indicate classroom and school consistent use of effective, efficient, and sustainable student-centered activities. The concept of creating a rubric from a district Mission for Student-Centered Twenty-First-Century Learning and Teaching for teachers and principals to use on a daily basis provides a tool for measuring if those activities are happening. There would be a need to create a data dashboard for activities grouped by classroom and school.

Perhaps you are starting to understand why the Mission for Student-Centered Twenty-First-Century Learning and Teaching must have a simple metric the teacher and principals can use on a daily basis to assess if their activities align with the organizational goals. It is the focal point of the organization's quality-management process.

We also know from current organizational-management research that mandating quality does not work. However, school districts are measured on the quality of their work as indicated by student achievement—what is the solution? Those same experts point out that management must create an environment where the members voluntarily adhere to the goals of the organization. The environment must enable members to manage their daily activities in alignment with the organization goals for those members of the organization. The teacher rubric enables that alignment.

Multiple organizational studies of both for-profit and nonprofit organizations indicate that if 30 percent of the members of the organization adopt change, the entire organization will change. The long-term goal is to have every teacher change to a student-centered learning environment.

However, if we can successfully engage 30 percent of your teachers in adopting this change, the remainder, representing the majority of your teachers, will follow and change also. Getting to a 30 percent penetration versus 100 percent is much more achievable.

Also incorporated in the book is information from corporate Europe and America regarding how IT organizations can be aligned with the organization's goals and brought into the organization, rather than being an isolated silo.

You have been thinking that these concepts do not apply to a school district. A school district is not a corporate organization, you are different. On one hand that is true, but on the other it is not. It is true that the primary goal of a for-profit corporation is to make a profit and that is not the primary goal of a school district. On the other hand, what current management theories are focusing on is the issue school districts are focusing on. The new curriculums, online assessments, and new teacher/principal evaluation systems are forcing school districts to address. How do we get people to adopt change?

How do we create a culture in the school district that encourages the majority of teachers and principals to change from a teacher-centered learning environment they are familiar with to an unfamiliar student-centered learning environment? You are missing the primary points of current organizational management and change management if you think a school district has nothing in common with corporate America. The concepts in this book are related to how we help the average human adopt change. From the viewpoint of creating a culture where people embrace change, there are no differences between profit-centered organizations and non-profit-centered organizations.

Those readers who have been or are engaged in curriculum and instruction within school districts have another question about this book. Where is the data? There have been too many trends adopted in schools without real data backing them up, or even studies with major flaws. If there is no data clearly indicating that a suggested process actually leads to improving in academic performance, you are not interested. So, "Where's the data?"

There are a large number of studies that clearly indicate that student-centered learning, in a wide variety of ranges, consistently results in dramatic improvement in student academic achievement. Teachers using one of those student-centered instructional delivery methodologies will see improvement in academic achievement. If you disagree that student-centered learning is a superior instructional delivery method, you have bigger issues. Your new state curriculum is extremely student-centered-learning oriented.

Your question should be: "Does the execution of the roadmap/operational plan generated by this process increase the number of teachers using student-centered learning experiences on a regular basis in their class-room?" Now you are connecting with the goal of this planning process. There are no studies to date; however, the anecdotal evidence is positive.

You may have found parts of the education sections weaker than the technology and facility sections. That is intentional, reflecting the reality that while student-centered learning is recognized as a superior instructional delivery method over traditional didactic delivery, there is little documentation of best practices. There is much debate but little comparative analysis that STEAM is better than STEM or PBL is superior to inquiry-based learning.

The majority of educational organizations are on a learning curve representing the first phase of adoption of a new inflection point. Few really have a firm grasp on what we would call best practices, indicating a superior methodology accomplishing specific goals, for student-centered learning. Hopefully you have been encouraged to take a higher-level viewpoint where your teachers and school-level administrators are encouraged to select which student-centered instructional delivery method they will use. Obviously there are limits to how far individual teacher flexibility of selection can go, but observing a wide variety of student-centered instructional delivery methods within a single facility indicates you have created a great culture of learning in your district.

This is a comprehensive, high-level framework that enables a school district to move from Point A—a teacher-centered learning culture—to somewhere closer to Point B—a student-centered learning and teaching culture. The multiple-silo concept and the coherent planning creating connections and conduits between the silos is what makes it powerful. The fact that everything is designed to relate back to "What and How Students Learn" should create a strong resonance with you. It bears repeating: the planning process is most efficient when all seven silos are included.

The word "submission" correctly has a negative connotation in our society. However, an earlier era used it in quite a different way. At that point in time, the word "submission" meant to place the interest of another person or group of people above your own interests. It was not the concept of superior and inferior position but a voluntary agreement to pursue the betterment of another person's condition ahead of improving your own personal condition.

The task of a truly competent consultant, someone selling his or her knowledge and understanding to others, is not to compete with clients, convincing them the consultant is right. The consultant's task is to adopt an attitude of submission and place the interests of the clients ahead of his or her own. If by chance aspects or concepts of this book have assisted or enlightened you to move toward a student-centered learning culture, we wish to respectfully join you in placing the interests of your students ahead of your own.

Appendix

SAMPLE "EFFECTIVE LEARNING AND TEACHING GAUGE"

This Gauge is designed to assist the planning-lab participants in developing a clear view of current level of penetration and participation associated with a number of issues pertaining to the silos of "What/How Students Learn" and "Professional Development."

DIRECTIONS:
- Each participant will complete this form as directed below without discussing the issue with the other participants in their respective group (discussion to clarify the issue is acceptable):
  - Address each issue from the viewpoint that the statement is true for what percentage of the identified group of people, in your opinion.
  - Use the following range of percentage indicators:
    - **1** = Minimal—The statement is true for less than 10 percent of the identified people.
    - **2** = Few—The statement is true for 10 percent to 25 percent of the identified people.
    - **3** = Some—The statement is true for 26 percent to 75 percent of the identified people.
    - **4** = Many—The statement is true for 76 percent to 90 percent of the identified people.
    - **5** = Most—The statement is true for 91 percent or more of the identified people.

- Upon completion of the form by each member in your group, your group will complete a second form as a group (method for determining scores or reaching consensus is at the group's discretion), and turn that group form into the facilitator.

What/How Students Learn

Score   Issue

VISION—Teachers and administrators understand that there is a district Vision for Twenty-First-Century Effective Learning and Teaching focused on best practices for student-centered leaning.

CONSISTENT VISION—Teachers and administrators believe that the district Vision for Twenty-First-Century Effective Learning and Teaching has been clearly articulated and communicated to the building level and classroom level within the district.

STUDENT LITERACY—Students have developed basic technology literacy and demonstrate mastery of skill sets appropriate for their grade level through assessments.

ACCESS TO TECHNOLOGY—Students have consistent access to technology, which enables them to develop technology literacy appropriate for their grade level.

STUDENT FLUENCY—Students have developed technology fluency and demonstrate mastery of those higher-order technology skill sets through assessments centered on activities where teachers have integrated technology into the activity and students are expected to determine their own path utilizing the appropriate application for the project.

TWENTY-FIRST-CENTURY EFFECTIVE LEARNING—Students consistently participate in Twenty-First-Century Effective Learning student-centered activities aligned to the state standards and with technology integration where appropriate.

UBIQUITOUS TECHNOLOGY—Students have technology available when and where they need it as a normal, everyday tool utilized as part of their instructional/learning process.

DATA-DRIVEN STUDENT LEARNING—All student activities that generate data regarding their knowledge/learning are downloaded into a database that is available in real time for teacher review and planning purposes.

Professional Development

TEACHERS HAVE BEEN TRAINED—Teachers have participated in training associated with best practices for Twenty-First-Century Effective Learning and Teaching.

TEACHERS UTILIZE TWENTY-FIRST-CENTURY TEACHING AND LEARNING—Teachers consistently utilize best practices for Twenty-First-Century Effective Teacher and Learning in their respective instructional environments.

PROFESSIONAL DEVELOPMENT CENTRALIZED—Teachers attend professional-development classes and events at a centralized location.

PROFESSIONAL DEVELOPMENT SITE BASED—Teachers attend professional-development classes and events in their respective buildings.

PROFESSIONAL DEVELOPMENT CLASSROOM BASED—Teachers participate in professional-development activities in their respective classrooms on an ad hoc basis when they need assistance.

TEACHER TECH LITERACY—Teachers have developed their basic technology literacy skill sets and are held accountable through an evaluation process to demonstrate those skills.

TEACHER TECH FLUENCY—Teachers have technology fluency that enables them to facilitate Twenty-First-Century Effective Learning and Teaching in their instructional space.

TEACHERS EVALUATED ON TWENTY-FIRST-CENTURY TEACHING AND LEARNING—Teachers are evaluated regarding their use of best practices of Twenty-First-Century Effective Learning and Teaching for student-centered activities in their instructional space.